Better Homes and Gardens®

HEIRLOOM EMBROIDERY

MURDOCH BOOKS®

Sydney • London • Vancouver • New York

Contents

4 Embroidered silk sachets

8 French embroidered bed linen

10 Wool embroidered blanket

14 Montmellick guest towels

18 French knot garden

22 Antique ivory christening set

26 Embroidered organza cushions

30 Nightgown with roses and daisies

32 Pansies and lace embroidered picture

36 Richelieu traycloth

38 Ribbon rose handkerchief sachet

42 Tree of life cross-stitch birth sampler

44 Blossom cross-stitched cushion

46 Pansy tablecloth

48 Bee and flower knot brooches

50 White iris evening bag

54 Shadow embroidered voile square

58 Hardanger table setting

62 Needlepoint bowl lid

64 Shadow embroidered coathanger

66 Honeycomb smocked nightdress

70 Cross-stitch garden picture

74 Lingerie bag with trapunto violets

78 Wreath of roses shoe stuffers

82 Candlewick wedding set

86 Caring for your embroidery

88 Materials and equipment

90 Stitch library

95 Index

Embroidered silk sachets

Each of these sachets uses different stitches and different coloured threads to produce effects that nonetheless blend together beautifully. Make all three, or choose your favourite design and make a matching set.

These beautiful silk sachets will give a touch of old-world luxury to your home when filled with dried lavender or potpourri. The simple floral designs are worked in stranded cotton using a variety of surface embroidery stitches.

Size Sachet 16 x 14 cm
Embroidery motifs On fold-out sheet F

Stitches

Bullion stitch
Detached chain stitch
Fly stitch
Long and short stitch
Stem stitch

Materials

For one sachet

- ◆ 46 x 17 cm of silk
- ◆ 46 x 17 cm of muslin (backing)

◄ Silks in subtle shades make a fine background for the delicate embroidery on these sachets. They will last for years and can be refilled whenever the scent fades.

- ◆ DMC stranded embroidery cottons in the following colours. *Spray design:* yellow-green (3347), light yellow-green (3348), dark yellow (726), light yellow (3078). *Ivy design:* dark pine green (3362), pistachio green (320), fern green (523), dark gold (830), light gold (833). *Wreath design:* green-grey (3052), salmon (760), light salmon (761), shell pink (225)
- ◆ 1 m of 4 mm wide green silk ribbon (for wreath sachet only)
- ◆ 1 m of ribbon (for bow)
- ◆ Small embroidery hoop
- ◆ Crewel needles size 7/9
- ◆ Lavender and small amount of toy fill
- ◆ Tracing paper
- ◆ Black pen
- ◆ Pencil or water-soluble pen

METHOD

1 Fold the fabric in half and press it lightly to mark the base line. Trace the design on fold-out sheet F onto tracing paper and tape it to a window or light box. Tape the fabric over it so that the design is above the crease and use a pencil or water-soluble pen to transfer the design to the fabric. If you prefer, draw on

The ivy design is worked mainly in long and short stitch.

the design freehand. The wreath is based on a circle 5.5 cm in diameter.

2 Baste the muslin to the wrong side of the silk. This is now treated as one piece of fabric. Zigzag or overlock all four sides.

3 Work the embroidery as follows, using the embroidery hoop.

■ *Spray.* Work the stems in stem stitch using yellow-green (3347), and using light yellow-green (3348) work the small leaves in detached chain stitch and the large leaves and calyx in fly stitch. To work the roses make three bullion stitches of five, six and seven twists using dark yellow (726) and then use light yellow (3078) to make two bullion stitches of eight twists either side. The buds are three bullion stitches of six twists, the inner in dark yellow and the two outer in light yellow. Use one strand of light green and one strand of dark green for the calyx; otherwise use two strands.

■ *Ivy.* Work the leaves and branch in long and short stitch. For the leaves use two strands of fern green and edge the four largest leaves in two strands of pistachio green. For the branch use one strand each of dark gold (830) and light gold (833). Work the stems in stem stitch, using one strand of dark pine green (3362) thread.

■ *Wreath.* The grub roses are worked with bullion stitch using three stitches of five twists for the centres, four stitches of six twists for the first round and five stitches of eight twists for the second round. Use light salmon for the centres and shell pink for the rounds. The buds are three bullion stitches of five twists, the centre one salmon and the other two light salmon. Work the stems in stem stitch, the leaves in detached chain stitch and the calyx in fly stitch, all in green-grey. Use one strand of green and two strands of the peach colours. The large leaves are worked in detached chain stitch and the green silk ribbon.

4 When the embroidery is complete, place the right sides of the fabric together and stitch the side seams. Turn down a 4 cm hem at the top and press.

5 Place lavender and a small amount of toy fill inside and tie with ribbon.

The wreath design is based on bullion stitches.

The spray design combines several surface embroidery stitches.

EARLY EMBROIDERY

Sewing with needle and thread is one of the earliest crafts practised by humans, who sewed together skins and later pieces of woven cloth to make garments. As these materials do not usually survive, the earliest definite evidence we have for sewing is indirect, but bone needles were in use in Europe by 20,000 BC. From the same period there are burials in which were found skeletons and rows of beads that had been sewn to garments.

The patterns in most early textiles were produced by weaving but beads and metal plaques were often stitched to garments, and one of the tunics in Tutankhamen's tomb (about 1450 BC) bore embroidered bands. It was possibly brought to Egypt from Syria. The Scythian tombs at Pazyryk in Siberia, dating from the fifth to third centuries BC, produced several embroideries. The Scythians, nomads who lived in eastern Europe and Russia, used beads, crystals and gold plaques sewn to clothing. Felt hangings and covers decorated with coloured felt appliqués in elaborate animal designs were also found, while a saddle cushion of silk embroidered with pheasants had perhaps come from China.

Embroidery, like other textile crafts, is usually done by women, but during the medieval period much fine embroidery was produced by male workers in professional workshops attached to monasteries. Most of it was for church use and the patterns and materials used could be very rich indeed: gold threads were often incorporated and the influence of manuscript illuminations was obvious. Noblewomen, too, produced a lot of rich embroideries during this period.

Secular embroideries produced during the medieval period included wall hangings, which are today often called 'tapestries' although tapestries are woven. The best known of these is the Bayeaux Tapestry, made to record the Norman conquest of England in 1066 and stitched with wool in eight colours (blues, greens, yellow and terracotta).

English needlework reached a peak during the medieval period, when ecclesiastical garments were covered in dense pictorial needlework in the technique known as *opus anglicanum*. This was worked in coloured silks, mostly in fine split stitch. The extremely high standard was also made possible by the development of couching from the underside, a process that allowed more flexibility in designs. *Opus anglicanum* flourished for about a hundred years, from 1250 until the Black Death severely reduced the embroidery workshops.

From about 1350 onwards elaborate embroideries depended less on skill and more on rich materials for their effect, and the designs became stiffer as they were influenced by woven tapestry. Among the techniques used was *or nué* ('shaded gold'), a technique in which gold threads were laid down horizontally and couched with coloured threads. Most areas of Europe now developed their own particular embroidery styles, used primarily for church vestments and royal regalia. Domestic embroidery did, of course, continue to be made throughout the medieval period, but we know little about it as few examples have been preserved.

The Reformation saw the production of elaborate church garments much reduced, at least in Protestant countries, and in England embroidery became very much a domestic and amateur activity mainly produced by noblewomen. This was the start of the heyday of domestic embroidery, when it was used extensively, especially on hangings and clothing. Characteristic was strapwork, a type of decoration that used interlaced curved or angular bands in regular patterns. It was derived from Moorish and oriental sources. Other favourite subjects were flowers and herbs, and mythological and Biblical subjects, many derived from pattern books, the first of which was produced in 1523.

Blackwork, or Spanish work, was a monochrome (usually black) form of embroidery that spread through Europe in the sixteenth century. It had been brought to Spain by the Moors. Blackwork made much use of strapwork and curving tendril designs, and Holbein stitch (double running stitch) was very popular.

French embroidered bed linen

Eyelet centres are used to lighten the heavier satin stitch petals.

Padded satin stitch decorates this bed linen, which is finished with a border of hem stitch. The style is known traditionally as French embroidery.

Finished size Pillowcase 73 x 48 cm
Embroidery motif On fold-out sheet C

Stitches

Buttonhole stitch
Cutwork eyelet stitch
Ladder hem stitch
Padded satin stitch
Stem stitch

Materials

- Sheet: white cotton in desired width and length, plus 14 cm
- Pillowcase: 1.80 m of 115 cm wide white cotton
- DMC embroidery cotton no. 20 in white (2 skeins for pillowcase and 3 skeins for sheet)
- White machine thread
- Sharp embroidery needle
- Dressmaker's carbon
- Tracing paper and sharp pencil

PILLOWCASE

1 Cut one piece 90 x 50 cm for the front and one piece 76 x 50 cm for the back.

2 On the front piece, mark a 57 x 31 cm frame with running stitches or pins. Position the frame 9.5 cm inside the long edges and the left-hand edge. Within this area, withdraw fabric threads over a width of 75 mm, cutting them 5 mm from the corners. Fold these thread ends to the back and finish the edges of the corner squares with small buttonhole stitches, using machine thread. Trim any ends at the back.

3 Work ladder hem stitch over the exposed threads, making bundles of six to eight fabric threads, depending on the thickness of the fabric.

4 Trace the daisy motif on fold-out sheet C onto tracing paper. Transfer it to the fabric with dressmaker's carbon. Position the design in the corner, inside the open hem stitch frame, about 3.5 cm from the top and left-hand sides. Work with one thread of embroidery cotton. Embroider the petals using padded satin stitch, the eyelets using cutwork eyelet stitch and the curls using stem stitch.

5 Hem the right side of both front and back with a 1 cm wide double hem. Place both pieces with right sides together and the left-hand edges even. Fold the extending part of the front over the back to form the casing and sew the left-hand edge and the two long edges together with 1 cm wide seams. Turn the pillowcase right side out.

SHEET

1 Baste a 6 cm wide double hem on one short side of the sheet.

2 Remove fabric threads over a width of 75 mm above the hem and work ladder hem stitch, securing the hem at the same time. Remove the basting.

3 Finish the remaining short side and the two long sides with 1 cm wide double hems.

4 Work the embroidery as for the pillowcase, positioning the design about 8 cm inside the hem stitch. Use the motif once, or extend the design by reversing it.

➤ *Hem stitching provides the ideal finish for this very special bed linen with French embroidery. Typical of this style of stitching is the combination of padded satin stitch and eyelets.*

Wool embroidered blanket

Angled straight stitches are used for the base leaves while a variety of other stitches are used to portray the varied textures and shapes of the flowers and foliage.

A variety of wools and surface stitches has been used to add texture and give an illusion of perspective to this whimsical garden scene. It turns a plain blanket into a real heirloom.

Finished size 110 x 80 cm
Embroidery motif On fold-out sheet A

Stitches
Back stitch
Bullion stitch
Chain stitch
French knot
Ladder stitch
Long-legged fly stitch
Split stitch
Stem stitch
Straight stitch

➤ *This charming cot blanket will keep baby warm and cosy, and the delicate appearance and soft colours of the wool ensure it will look at home in any nursery. A stem stitch border (not shown) is worked around the edge of the binding to suggest piping.*

This old-fashioned cottage garden—complete with ladybirds and a buzzing bee—is a delightful decoration for any blanket. Here it is embroidered on a cot blanket but it would look equally pretty on a small rug.

Materials

- 1.10 x 0.80 m of cream wool blanketing
- 1.40 m of fabric backing
- 50 x 35 cm of stiff tulle
- Water-soluble pen
- Black or blue permanent marker pen
- Crewel embroidery needle size 9
- Little Woods 3-ply gross mohair in variegated green
- Little Woods 3-ply variegated blue
- Appleton crewel wool in olive green (341), pine green (352), forest green (401), dark pink (754), medium pink (753), light pink (751), mauve (886), yellow (471 and 841) and blue (743)
- DMC stranded embroidery cotton in cream (677), red (347) and grey (645)
- Machine thread in cream

THE BASE LEAVES

1 Transfer the pattern on fold-out sheet A to the tulle using a permanent marker pen. Let it dry. The tulle becomes your stencil.

2 Centre the tulle on the blanketing, about 35 cm from the bottom. Using the water-soluble pen, draw in the leaves at the base of the design. At this stage draw only the leaves as they are embroidered first.

3 Using the variegated green mohair wool and stem stitch, embroider the stem of a leaf and the vein. Then fill in the leaf shape with straight stitches angled to give a 'realistic' effect. Embroider the remaining leaves but start each with a part of the wool that is a different colour so that each leaf is different.

4 When the leaves are all embroidered, use a damp cloth to remove the marks of the pen. Do this at each stage of your embroidery. Mark and embroider only one section at a time.

THE FLOWERS

1 Replace the tulle and draw the cow parsley and spokes, although there is no need to draw the French knots of the flower head. Using Appleton olive green (341) embroider the stem in stem stitch and the spokes with long-legged fly stitches, placing an extra stitch in the centre of each one. To form the flower head use Appleton mauve (886) and embroider as many French knots of two twists as are needed to make a really neat shape.

2 Mark and embroider the second cow parsley in the same way.

3 Mark the cream grasses and then embroider them in stem stitch using three strands of cream embroidery cotton (677), and using French knots (three twists) for the seeds.

4 Mark the solid leaf shapes and embroider them in split stitch using Appleton pine green (352). Work from the base of the leaf. Use stem stitch and one strand of wool for the stem.

5 Mark the yellow daisies. The stems are embroidered in chain stitch with one strand of Appleton pine green (352). The flowers are worked with straight stitches in four strands of Appleton yellow (841). Keep a loose tension for a rounded effect. The centres are worked in French knots (one twist) using one strand of Appleton yellow (471). Using one strand of Appleton forest green (401) work the stems of the leaves in stem stitch and the leaves in long-legged fly stitches with an extra centre stitch.

6 Mark the bluebells. The stems and leaves are in stem stitch using one strand of Appleton forest green (401). The calyx is formed by working three small straight stitches into the same hole and four straight stitches out from the calyx. See the diagram for their placement. Work the bluebell around the calyx using two strands of variegated blue. Use straight stitches from the end of the calyx, then work two shorter stitches on each side to create the illusion of a bell. The buds are worked with three stitches.

7 Mark the pink flower. The stem is embroidered with one strand of variegated green in stem stitch. The leaves are three straight stitches with the central one slightly longer than the others. Work the flower buds at the top using one strand of dark pink (754) and three tiny straight stitches. Then use three strands of light pink (751) and straight stitches to embroider three small flowers with five petals. Keep the tension loose. Below them, work six flowers in medium pink (753) and then below them eight in dark pink (754). The centres are all a French knot with one twist worked with one strand of light pink.

8 Mark the small pink flower stem and work in the same way, using the light and medium pinks for the buds. Mix the colours to make it interesting. Work the flowers scattered among the base leaves in the three shades of pink with the centres in light pink, as for the pink flowers.

LADYBIRDS AND BEE

1 Mark the three ladybirds, one on the split stitch leaf, one on the tallest daisy and one on the stem of grass. The ladybird body is created in a V shape. Use two strands of red embroidery cotton (347) and work eight straight stitches into the same hole, four on each side to make the wings. Using grey (645) fill the body with four straight stitches and make three small straight stitches across the top to form the head. Use a French knot, one twist, to make the dots on the wings and one strand of cotton and two straight stitches to add the feelers.

2 Mark the bee. The body consists of four rows of bullion stitches with a small space between each row. Use one strand of Appleton yellow (471) with ten twists and make the stitch 3–4 mm wide so that the bullion curves. Using three strands of grey embroidery cotton (645), fill the spaces with bullion stitches with ten twists, except the stitch at the tip of the body which has only five twists. Using three strands of grey, make the head from a bullion stitch of twenty twists, placed in a semi-circle and caught down with one strand of thread. Again using one strand of grey, add two straight stitches to make the feelers and sew the wings with back stitch.

BACKING AND BINDING THE BLANKET

1 Measure the blanket and make sure it is cut straight and even. Cut the backing 11 cm longer and wider than the blanket to allow for a 4 cm turn all around and 1.5 cm seam allowances. Press in the seam allowance and then the 4 cm turn.

2 Slip the blanket into the backing with right sides outwards. Trim the corners to allow the corners of the backing to be neatly mitred. Pin and tack the pieces together and ladder stitch the corners.

3 If you have a blind hem stitch foot on your machine, use it for the top stitching on the blanket. Place the blade at the edge of the fabric and the needle at the far right. Keep the blade evenly on the edge of the fabric as you sew so as to produce an even, professional-looking top stitching.

4 Using one strand of Appleton blue (743), embroider stem stitch around the edge of the fabric trim. Do not put the needle through to the backing but stitch just through the blanketing. Sink the beginning and end of the wool neatly into the hem.

Montmellick guest towels

The traditional Montmellick foliage patterns are re-created here using equally traditional heavy cotton thread on shiny cotton fabric.

White-on-white Montmellick embroidery was developed in 1825 in Montmellick village, County Waterford, Ireland by Johanna Carter. Here traditional stitches and patterns are used to create a truly luxurious pair of guest towels.

Finished size Towel 56 x 39 cm; embroidered panel 6 cm wide
Embroidery motifs On fold-out sheet A

Stitches

Braid stitch
Bullion stitch
Buttonhole fringe
Buttonhole stitch
Cable stitch
Chain stitch
Coral knot stitch
Double feather stitch
Double knot stitch
French knot
Herringbone stitch
Honeycomb stitch
Overcast stitch
Satin stitch
Split stitch
Stem stitch
Trellis stitch with spider web
Whipped stem stitch

Materials

- 70 cm of waffle cotton
- 20 cm of cotton sateen
- DMC Coton à Broder 12 Blanc (5 skeins)
- DMC Coton à Broder 20 Blanc (1 skein)
- Crewel needles sizes 3/9
- Straw needle size 3
- Rectangle roller stretcher frame
- Tracing paper
- Black pen
- Fine-tip water-soluble marker pen
- Machine thread

PREPARATION

1 Pre-shrink and press both fabrics before cutting out the towels.

➤ *Blackberries and acorns are traditional motifs for Montmellick embroidery and are used here to give an authentic touch to these two beautiful waffle weave hand towels.*

A buttonhole fringe gives the finishing touch to each of the towels. This one has the blackberry border.

2 Cut two pieces of cotton sateen 10 x 47 cm. Trace the design on fold-out sheet A, including the hem lines, onto tracing paper using the black pen. Tape the tracing paper to a window or light box. Centre the sateen over the tracing with the right side facing you and tape it in position. Lightly trace the design with the water soluble pen. Remove the sateen.

3 Centre one piece of sateen in the stretcher frame. Lace it with a strong thread until it is taut and embroider the first border. Use the crewel needles for all stitches except for the bullion work.

BLACKBERRY BORDER

1 Embroider the stem in cable stitch, using Broder 12 for the main (horizontal) stem and Broder 20 for the side stems.

2 Using Broder 12 outline the flower petals in split stitch and pad them with chain stitch. Work satin stitch over this and fill the centre of the flower with French knots with two twists around the needle. The small flower is worked in the same way but using Broder 20.

3 Using Broder 12 fill in the berry shapes with French knots with two twists. The sepals are worked in satin stitch using Broder 20.

4 Work the leaves as follows. Outline leaf 1 in coral knot stitch and work the veins in double feather stitch with Broder 12. Embroider one half of leaf 2 in honeycomb stitch using Broder 20 and outline it in whipped stem stitch with Broder 12; the other half of the leaf is outlined with split stitch, padded with chain stitch and worked in satin stitch, using Broder 12 for both stitches. Leaf 3 is outlined in double knot stitch and the centre veins are worked in braid stitch using Broder 12.

ACORN BORDER

1 This border is embroidered entirely in Broder 12. Work the stems in overcast stitch, using two strands for the core and one strand for the overcasting.

2 Outline the acorns in split stitch, pad them with chain stitch and then use satin stitch over this. Fill the acorn cup with French knots worked with two twists.

3 For leaf 1, lay the threads for the trellis at a 45 degree angle and sew them down with a small stitch where they cross. Then weave spider web over and under the crossing threads three times. Outline the leaf in whipped stem stitch.

4 Embroider the outside edge of leaf 2 in buttonhole stitch and do the centre vein with stem stitch. Using the straw needle, work pairs of bullion stitches out from the centre vein.

5 Outline one half on leaf 3 and the centre vein with stem stitch. Fill in the space with herringbone stitch.

The acorn border is shown here, along with the buttonhole fringe. The loops of the fringe must not be cut or it will unravel.

Work a row of French knots, with two twists around the needle, down the outside of the stem stitch. Work the outline of the other half of the leaf in split stitch, then pad it with chain stitch and finally work it in satin stitch.

TO ASSEMBLE TOWELS

1 Cut two pieces of waffle cotton 65 x 43 cm. Turn up a 5 cm hem on the bottom (one short end) of the towel and press.

2 Remove the embroidery from the stretcher frame and trim 1 cm out from the lines. Turn in the 1 cm seams and press.

3 Centre the embroidery on the towel, over the hem, with the bottom 4 cm up from the bottom of the towel. Pin it in place and machine stitch both edges.

4 Tack a line with sewing thread 5 mm up from the lower edge of the border as a guide for the buttonhole fringe and a line 3 mm in from the top edge as a guide for the buttonhole border.

5 Embroider the buttonhole border along the top edge of the embroidered strip, using buttonhole stitch and Broder 12.

6 Along the lower edge of the embroidered strip, work the buttonhole fringe using Broder 12. To do this, you will need a very long length of thread. Work one buttonhole stitch on the edge of the fold. Insert the needle at the top of this stitch and then bring it down under your left thumb for about 2 cm so as to form the first loop. Insert the needle beside the first buttonhole stitch and work a second stitch. Make the second loop and repeat the sequence. Finish securely to prevent the fringe unravelling. Take note, too, that the loops on a buttonhole fringe must never be cut or it will unravel.

Buttonhole fringe

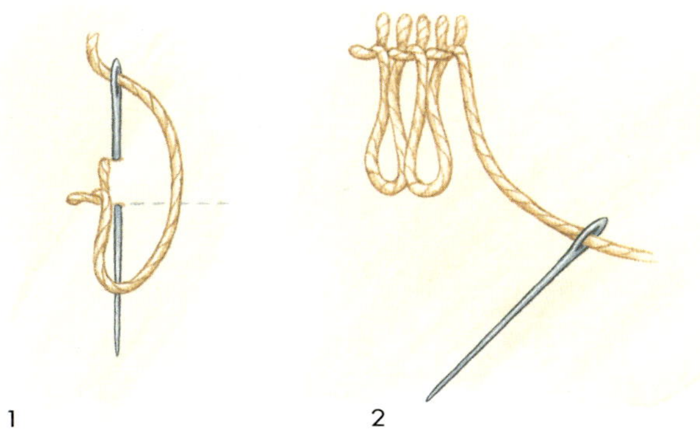

TO FINISH

1 Machine a double 1 cm hem along the other short end of the towel and then down the long sides but be careful not to continue the machine stitching through the embroidered strip.

2 Slip stitch the hem by hand.

French knot garden

A riot of colours fills the beds of this knot garden, and the brilliant effect is achieved with only two stitches—French knots and stem stitch.

Embroidery worked entirely, or almost entirely, in French knots has become almost a genre in itself. This witty design takes a French knot picture and adds a Celtic knot design in the centre.

Finished size Embroidered panel 15 x 14 cm
Pattern On fold-out sheet C

Stitches

French knot
Stem stitch

Materials

- 40 x 40 cm of Zweigart congress cloth art. 9406, colour 294
- Straw needles size 3/9
- Tapestry needle size 24
- DMC stranded embroidery cottons in the following colours: violet (327); antique violet (3042); antique mauve (3727); dusty rose (3354); dark dusty rose (3731); red (350); light red (351); pistachio green (320); light pistachio green (368); very light pistachio green (369); fern green (523); light fern green (524); gold (676); tangerine (741); light tangerine (742); yellow (743); light sky blue (747); sky blue (3761); very dark cornflower blue (791); dark cornflower blue (792); cornflower blue (793); brown (829); light brown (3045)
- DMC Coton Perlé no. 8 in light pistachio green (368)
- Hoop or embroidery frame
- HB pencil
- Masking tape

METHOD

The garden is made up of four sections, A, B, C and D. The flowers are embroidered in French knots, working across one bar of canvas in any direction.

Stem stitch is used for the Celtic knot and the edge of each section of garden. The outside frame consists of two rows of stem stitch. The straight lines of the stem stitch are embroidered across two threads of the canvas, returning the needle to the hole of the last stitch to form a straight, thin line. On the curve of the garden edge and the Celtic knot you need to place the stem stitch so that it makes an even edge.

STEM STITCH EMBROIDERY

1 Prepare the cloth by taping the edges with masking tape. Measure in 19 cm from the side and 16 cm from the top of the canvas, and mark. This is the starting point. See the pattern on fold-out sheet C.

2 Starting from the marked point, work the stem stitch border around section A. Use the tapestry needle and Coton Perlé. Work up the short side over twenty threads, then across the top over fifty threads, then down the long side over fifty-six threads, and finally across the fourth side (the short side) over twenty threads.

3 Use a light box or tape both the canvas and design onto a window and then trace off the curve to complete the edging of section A. Work stem stitch over the curve.

4 Work the outlines of sections B, C and D in the same way, leaving ten threads between each section.

5 Using a light source as above, transfer the Celtic knot design to the canvas, making sure it is centred accurately. Embroider it in stem stitch, using the tapestry needle and Coton Perlé. Start at the point marked with an 'x' on the design and work in one direction until you reach the starting point. Stitch five or six rows of stem stitch to cover the design.

This picture is truly a masterpiece that will amply reward stitchers with the patience to complete it. The gardens full of flowers are worked in French knots, while garden edgings, border and the Celtic knot in the centre are all added in stem stitch.

FRENCH KNOT EMBROIDERY

Embroider the gardens with French knots, using the stranded embroidery cottons and the smallest size of straw needle that you can manage. Using a straw needle makes it easier to get a tight, neat knot. See the photographs on pages 20–1 and the following detailed instructions.

Section A

Area 1: deep pink flowers. Two strands 3731 and one strand 3354 with two twists and six to eight knots in each circle. Centres: two strands of 829 with one twist and three or four knots to fill the centre.

Area 2: pink flowers. Two strands of 3354 and one strand of 3727 with two twists and six to eight knots in each circle. Centres: two strands of 327 with one twist and one to three knots to fill the centre.

Area 3: mauve flowers. Two strands of 3042 and one strand of 327 with two twists and six to eight knots in each circle. Centres: two strands of 676 with two twists and two to five knots to fill the centre.

Area 4: deep blue flower. Base of flower three strands of 791 with two twists and ten to twelve knots. Above: two strands of 792 and one strand of 3042 with two twists and six to eight knots in each circle. Centres: two strands of 791 with three twists and two to four knots to fill the centre. Fill in around the flowers with two strands of 3042 with one twist.

Area 5: light blue flowers. Some flowers of two strands of 3761 and one strand of 747 with two twists and six to eight knots in each circle; and some flowers of two strands of 747 with two twists and six to eight knots in each circle. Centres: two strands of 676 with two twists and one knot.

Section A

Section B

Area 6: red flowers. Two strands of 350 with two twists and six to eight knots in each circle; tiny flowers a single knot. Centres: two strands of 829 with two twists and two knots.

Background: greens. Use single knots with one twist. Left side: splatter around area to left of blue flowers knots of one strand 369 and one strand 523, then fill in with knots of two strands of 369. Centre: two strands 369. Right side: two strands 368.

Section B

Area 1: deep blue flowers. Two strands 792 and one strand 3042 with two twists and six to eight knots in circle. Centres: two strands 791 with three twists and two to five knots to fill centre. Fill in around flowers with two strands of 3042 with one twist.

Area 2: light blue flowers. Worked with two twists and six to eight knots in a circle, some flowers in two strands 3761 and one strand 747, and some in two strands 747. Centres: two strands 676 with two twists and one to three knots to fill centre.

Area 3: red flowers. Three strands 350 with two twists and six to eight knots in a circle; tiny flowers two twists and single knot. Centres: two strands 829 with two twists and two to six knots to fill centre.

Area 4: yellow flowers. Darker flowers: two strands 743 and one strand 741 with two twists and eight to eighteen knots in a circle. Centres: two strands 351 with two twists and two to four knots to fill circle. Lighter flowers: two strands 743 with two twists and six to eight knots in a circle. Centres: two strands 742 with two twists and two to four knots to fill centre.

Area 5: light blue flowers. Two strands 747 with two twists in groups of three to four knots, and three strands 3761 with two twists. Embroider a few knots on top to give the area texture.

Background: greens. Left side: fill in area around purple flower with knots of two strands of 368 with one twist and area around blue flowers with knots of one twist using one strand of 368 and one of 369. Top right: fill area at top of red flowers with knots of one twist using one strand of 524 and one strand of 523, and area at base of red flowers with knots of two twists using two strands of 369. In the centre work a solid area with knots of one twist using two strands of 369, and fill the rest of the area with sprinklings of the same and highlights of knots of one twist using two strands of 368 or one strand of 369.

Section C

Area 1: brown area. Splatter across the lower part knots of one or two twists using two strands of 3045 and two of 829. Fill the area with knots of one twist using two strands of 3045.

Area 2: red flowers. Three strands of 350 with two twists and six to eight knots in a circle; tiny flowers two twists and a single knot. Centres: two strands of 829 with one twist and three to five knots to fill the centre.

Area 3: orange flowers. Two flowers of two strands of 351 and one strand of 741 with two twists and eight to ten knots in a circle; centres two strands of 3045 with two twists and three to five knots to fill the centre. Top flower: two strands of 742 and one strand of 741 with two twists and eight to ten knots in a circle; centre: two strands of 351 with two twists and three to four knots to fill the centre.

Section C

Section D

Area 4: pink flowers. Three strands of 3354 with two twists, five to ten knots in a clump and single knots.
Area 5: yellow flowers. Three strands 743 with two twists and eight to ten knots in a clump. Tiny flowers extend down into area 1: two strands 743 and two strands 741 with two twists.
Area 6: orange flower. Two strands 741 and one strand 351 with two twists and eight knots to form circle. Centre: two strands 742 with two twists.
Area 7: light blue flowers. Three strands 3761 with two twists and six to eight knots in a circle. Centre: two strands 743 with two twists and one to three knots to fill centre.
Area 8: green leaves. Two strands of 320 with two twists, grouped to look like leaves.
Area 9: light blue flowers. Three strands of 747 with two twists; groups of three or four knots scattered over area. Highlight groups with knots of two twists using three strands of 3761.
Background: greens. Bottom left corner and up curved edge: cover with knots of one twist using one strand 523 and one strand 524. Lower middle area: cover area solidly with knots of one twist using two strands 369. Middle area: fill with knots of one twist using one strand of 369.

Section D

Area 1: red flowers. Three strands 350 or 351 with two twists and six to eight knots in circle; tiny flowers two twists and single knot. Centres: two strands 829 with two twists and three to five knots to fill centre.
Area 2: deep pink flowers. Two strands 3731 and one strand 3354 with two twists and six to eight knots in circle. Centre: two strands 829 with two twists and two to four knots to fill centre.
Area 3: yellow pansies. Centre: in a triangle, place three knots of two twists using two strands 829. Fill in around them with knots of two twists using three strands of 676.
Area 4: brown area. Scatter knots of two twists using two strands of 829 and two strands of 3045. Fill in with knots of one twist using two strands of 3045.
Area 5: deep blue and violet flowers. Place knots of two twists using three strands of 793 in groups or singly. Add groups of knots of two twists using three strands of 327 across the base.
Area 6: pink flowers. Over this whole area work groups of four knots using two twists and two strands of 3354. Add groups of three knots using two twists and two strands of 3727. Splatter over area knots with two twists using one strand 3727 and one strand 792, and then using one strand 3731 and one strand 3354.
Background: greens. Left side: Splatter over area knots of one twist using one strand 369 and one strand 523. Fill in with knots of one twist using three strands 320. Middle section: Solid area of knots of one twist using one strand 523 and one strand 524. Under this solid area work knots of two twists using three strands 320 arranged to look like leaves. Lower section: Splatter around knots of one twist using two strands of 523.

TO FINISH

Work a border of two rows of stem stitch around the picture, placing it ten threads outside the French knot gardens. To make neat corners, catch the thread at the back at each corner and restart for the next side.

Antique ivory christening set

Tiny flowers and tendrils make a delicate embroidery motif.

Worked on an ivory cotton voile for a rich, antique feel, this christening gown and bonnet will quickly become a true family heirloom. The design has been adapted to make a matching hanger for the gown, embroidered with the same flowers and a bow executed in shadow work.

Size Can be adapted to any gown and bonnet size; hanger 30 cm long
Embroidery motifs On fold-out sheet B

Stitches

Back stitch
Colonial knot
Detached chain stitch
Double back stitch
Ladder stitch
Stem stitch
Straight stitch

Materials

- Commercial pattern for gown and bonnet (we adapted Style 2436 size A)
- Ivory cotton voile
- Matching machine thread
- Lace, ribbon and buttons as required by the pattern
- DMC stranded embroidery cotton in off-white (746) (3 skeins)
- Tracing paper
- HB pencil
- Quilting needle size 10
- Mill Hill Glass Seed Beads in cream (00123)

Hanger

- 30 cm wooden hanger
- Embroidery hoop
- 1.5 m ivory satin piping
- 20 cm plastic piping 0.5 mm
- 20 cm Pellon
- 50 cm medium wadding
- 1 m of 3 mm wide ivory ribbon

THE GOWN

The embroidery on the yoke is worked before the yoke is cut out; that on the skirt can be worked before or after the gown is completed but for a double row of designs you will need a hem 9 cm deep. You will probably need to add to the length when cutting out.

1 Trace the front yoke pattern onto a generous rectangle of the fabric but do not cut it out until after you have finished the embroidery.
2 Cut out the front and back of the skirt as directed, lengthening it as necessary to achieve a 9 cm hem. Cut out the remaining pieces of the pattern.
3 Trace the yoke pattern onto a sheet of tracing paper and use this to plan the placement of the embroidery motifs. The motifs are on fold-out sheet B. Trace them onto the yoke pattern, ensuring they do not extend into the seam areas. We used five motifs on the yoke, all placed vertically, two on either side and one in the centre. You can vary the placement as you like and to suit your pattern.
4 Tape the tracing paper pattern to a window or light box, tape the front yoke fabric over it and trace off the design using the HB pencil. Use a short line to indicate the flower petals.
5 Around the hem we used a double row of horizontally placed motifs. Trace the motifs from the fold-out sheet onto tracing paper and transfer it to the front skirt in the same way as for the yoke. Repeat the motifs as necessary and adjust the space between motifs so that they fit neatly. Remember to allow for the side seams and the hem. Repeat on the back skirt, making sure it matches.

➤ *The embroidery on this beautiful christening set can be adapted to suit any gown and bonnet, as the design can be placed upright or sideways and repeated as often as you want.*

The dainty motifs and subtle ivory-on-ivory scheme combine to produce a christening gown of special quality.

6 Use one strand of embroidery cotton in the quilting needle. Start the flowers by working a few small back stitches in the centre (they will be covered by the seed bead). For each petal work three straight stitches in and out of the same hole, keeping a fairly loose tension, and then edge them with a detached chain stitch. A seed bead is added to the centre of the flower with two stitches to hold it in place. Finish off at the back with two colonial knots. Embroider each flower separately.

Just a few of the embroidered motifs are all it takes to make a matching bonnet to complete the set.

7 Starting with a waste knot, embroider the stem and leaves using stem stitch for the stems and detached chain stitch for the leaves, catching the thread at the back as much as possible to avoid dragging it across the fabric as the voile is quite transparent. The neater the embroidery, the nicer the finish. Weave the thread ends neatly into the back of the embroidery.

8 When all embroidery is finished, cut out the yoke and assemble the gown following the pattern instructions. All lace was hand stitched to the gown.

THE BONNET

1 Cut out the bonnet. Trace the motifs onto it as for the gown. We placed five motifs around the front, one in the centre and two on either side.

2 Complete the embroidery as for the gown and then assemble the bonnet.

THE HANGER

1 Following the pattern on fold-out sheet B, make a paper pattern for the hanger. Transfer the pattern to the voile, placing the piece for the front on the bias and the piece for the back on the straight grain. Do not cut out the pieces at this stage. Seam allowances of 6 mm are included in the pattern.

A shadow work bow is the main motif on this hanger, while the embroidered flowers link it to the gown and bonnet.

2 Trace the design for the bow onto the front piece. Do not trace the flowers at this stage. Place the fabric into the embroidery hoop.

3 The shadow work is embroidered on the right side of the fabric using a double back stitch and one strand of embroidery cotton in the quilting needle. Always start with a waste knot. Bring the needle to the front approximately 2 mm from the tip of the ribbon ends, then back to the tip. Continue stitching from side to side making small back stitches. On the curves you will need to adjust the stitches, making smaller stitches on the inside curve and larger stitches on the outside curve.

4 After the bow is completed, trace the flowers onto the fabric, using little straight lines for the petals. Embroider them as for the gown.

5 Cut a 20 cm piece of satin piping to cover the hook of the hanger. Unpick it, discard the cord, press the fabric flat, fold it in half and sew a 6 mm seam down the length of the fabric to make a tube 1.2 cm wide. If the piping did not have a generous seam allowance you may have to join two pieces to make an equivalent tube. Trim excess off the top. Turn right side out. Cut the plastic piping to fit the hook, slip the satin tube over the piping so that it fits snugly. Trim the fabric to 5 mm at the base of the plastic tube and push the fabric ends into it. Push the plastic tube over the hook until it sits flat on the wood.

6 Lay the embroidery face down on a thick towel and iron it carefully. Cut out the front and back and cut two pieces of Pellon the same size. Pin one piece of Pellon to the wrong side of the front. With the raw edges even, pin the piping to the right side, starting at the hook with a bit of overlap at the end of the piping. Curve the piping evenly around the edge of the fabric, making small snips in the bias around the curves. Stitch along the stitching on the piping and across the overlap section.

7 Pin the second piece of Pellon to the wrong side of the back and stitch across the lower edge. With right sides together and raw edges matching, pin the front to the back and tack them together. Starting at the centre top (but leaving space for the hook) stitch along the top and around the end. Repeat on the other side. Do not stitch across the bottom.

8 Cut the wadding to an 8 cm strip and starting at the hook, wrap it firmly around the hanger. Place an extra piece of wadding at the ends. Repeat this two or three times, using a slip stitch where necessary to hold it in place. Repeat on the other end of the hanger. The result should be firm and even, with no lumps.

9 Place the padded hanger in the cover. You may need to stuff extra wadding into the ends. Pin the edges together and ladder stitch the opening closed. Cut two 50 cm lengths of 3 mm wide ribbon and tie a double bow around the hook.

Embroidered organza cushions

Shadow work is used to create the repeated leaf designs used on one of the cushions. The bright colour has considerable impact but the design would be equally effective if it were worked in somewhat softer tones.

The repeated designs and strong colours of these lovely embroidered organza cushions convey the essence of modern design while looking so beautiful they will quickly become treasured heirlooms. Use them to give a touch of luxury to any room.

Finished size Cushion 38 x 38 cm; embroidered panel 30 x 30 cm
Embroidery motifs On fold-out sheet C

Stitches

Chain stitch
Closed herringbone stitch
Running stitch

Materials

- 1 m of ivory polyester organza
- 1 m ivory silk

➤ *Repeated designs embroidered on organza can look so up-to-the-minute. The stitches are simple, some worked on the right side of the fabric and some on the back.*

- DMC stranded embroidery cotton in the following colours: beige (543), light parrot green (907), aquamarine (992) and 2 skeins kelly green (702)
- Quilting needle size 7
- Sewing thread
- Tracing paper, pencil and ruler
- Embroidery hoop

PREPARATION

1 Cut six pieces of organza 40 x 40 cm. Make a paper pattern 30 x 30 cm. Pin it to the centre of one piece of organza and work running stitches around the outside. Remove the paper and repeat on two other pieces of organza. These will be the cushion fronts.
2 Copy the motifs on fold-out sheet C onto tracing paper. Transfer them to the prepared fronts, scattering them as desired but leaving free a 2 cm border inside the frame. Use the ruler to space the motifs evenly. Place the organza, right side up, on top of the tracing and trace the outlines gently with a sharp, soft pencil, taking care not to shift the fabric. The motifs can be traced after the organza is in the embroidery hoop.

EMBROIDERY

Gently stretch the organza in the embroidery hoop. The embroidery is worked with one long strand of cotton folded double, forming a loop at the end of the thread. To start the embroidery, insert the needle from the wrong side of the work, make a small back stitch on the right side and insert the needle through the loop of the cotton at the wrong side. This gives a clean, knot-free start. When the motif is completed, lace away the thread ends into the existing embroidery at the wrong side of the fabric, taking care that it will not show through on the right side. Do not carry the thread over to the next motif.

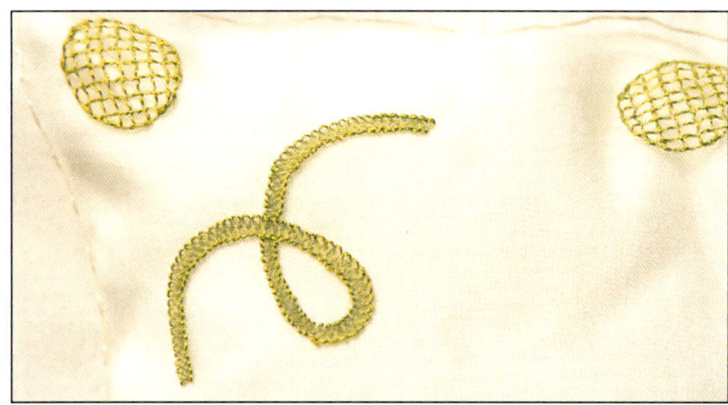

Closed herringbone stitch and running stitch are used to create the design of circles and curls used on this bright cushion.

The flowers on this cushion are worked in chain and running stitches, the simplicity of the stitching reflecting the simple shapes.

Work the cushions in the following way:

■ *Flower cushion.* Stitch the outlines of the flowers in chain stitch and the circles in running stitch, working on the right side of the fabric using aquamarine (992).

■ *Circles and curls cushion.* In light parrot green (907), stitch the circles using small running stitches on the right side of the fabric, and the curls in closed herringbone stitches worked from the wrong side of the fabric, showing a double line of back stitches on the right side with the 'shadow' of the herringbone stitches appearing between them.

■ *Leaves cushion.* Using kelly green (702), work closed herringbone stitches from the wrong side of the fabric, showing a double line of back stitches on the right side with the 'shadow' of the herringbone stitches appearing between them.

TO MAKE UP THE CUSHIONS

1 Cut six pieces of silk 32 x 32 cm. Pin them together in pairs with right sides together (1 cm seams are allowed). Stitch around, leaving a 10 cm opening. Clip the corners and turn through. Press. Place inserts into the silk envelope; slip stitch the opening closed.
2 Press the embroidered pieces to remove creases. Pin each to an organza square with right sides together and 1 cm seams. Stitch, leaving a 10 cm opening in one side. Ensure edges are neat. Turn and press.
3 Measure in 4 cm from each edge and mark with pins. With three strands of beige (543), stitch running stitches, leaving a 10 cm opening to correspond to that in the outer edge. Do not cut off the thread.
4 Insert cushion into the centre and complete the running stitches. Slip stitch the outer opening closed.

EMBROIDERY: THE LAST 400 YEARS

The seventeenth century saw a surge in the popularity of wall hangings and upholstered furniture, and this had a profound effect on the types of embroidery most commonly practised. Embroidery forms that resulted in strong, hard-wearing materials became popular, notably canvas work and crewel work.

Crewel work had developed in England in the previous century and now reached its peak there and in the American colonies (it is sometimes known as Jacobean embroidery). Crewel work is a type of freestyle embroidery worked in two-ply worsted wool on linen or cotton cloth, and it is characterised by its graceful designs and beautiful colours. The intricate designs were time-consuming to stitch but the background was left unstitched. The designs developed out of those used for sixteenth century blackwork and were strongly influenced by the oriental designs that became familiar as trade with India and the East increased. Luxuriant foliage patterns and landscapes with rocky or hilly ground were typical. Most surface embroidery stitches were used, including trellis and honeycomb filling and a range of couched stitches.

The stitching of small panels and pictures was popular and they were often worked in tent stitch or coloured beadwork. By the middle of the century small pieces were also made in stumpwork. This padded embroidery, which was often encrusted with seed pearls, developed from the padded work on European church vestments.

In the eighteenth century embroidery was regarded as a serious amateur pursuit for women and even some men. Canvas work became the predominant form, usually worked in tent and cross stitches in wool with silks for highlighting. The bold designs included floral, chinoiserie, Biblical and mythological motifs, and portraits were also popular. Crewel work was still popular, especially in the early part of the century, and very fine crewel work was done now in America.

The nineteenth century saw a huge increase in the amount of embroidery produced as the large middle classes created by the Industrial Revolution took to this pastime with fervour. At the same time, embroidery also felt the effects of the standardisation characteristic of the period. Pictures, often worked in long and short stitches using wools and silks, were very popular.

From the 1830s the phenomenon of Berlin woolwork flourished and quickly became by far the most common form of embroidery. Early forms were sometimes worked in silk on fine canvas, but the use of wool and a coarser canvas soon became standard as they were easier to work with and less expensive. Tent and cross stitches were used. The stitcher followed a printed chart, hand-coloured by women working in publishers' warehouses. These charts depicted an enormous range of subjects, with flowers and animals particularly popular. Soft colours were used until the introduction of aniline chemical dyes led to the adoption of bright ones. Backgrounds were often dark, and black was common. Silks were used for highlighting and beads were added to give texture.

The nineteenth century also saw the introduction of machine-made embroidery. In 1828 a multi-needle embroidery machine was invented by Josué Heilmann of Mulhouse in France and by the 1850s machine embroidery was being produced commercially. The designs were naturally repetitive but the process was accurate and the resulting embroidery was affordable.

The later nineteenth century saw the appearance of Art Needlework, a reaction against the perceived dullness of Berlin woolwork. It copied the forms that were used in drawing and painting. Many schools and societies were set up to promote needlework of this type and designs were created by a number of artists. William Morris was prominent in the movement, and he and his followers drew inspiration for many of their designs from the past, especially the medieval period. Crewel work also enjoyed renewed popularity as part of this movement.

The trends during this century have been less obvious, but many old forms have been adapted to suit modern tastes, and machine embroidery has a strong following. Kits, complete with design and materials, are particularly popular.

Nightgown with roses and daisies

Sprays of bullion roses and clusters of daisies worked in detached chain stitch embellish this white satin nightdress.

The heavy, richness of bullion stitches shows to advantage on this nightgown. They are named for their resemblance to the finely coiled gold wire used in early embroideries.

Embroidery motif On fold-out sheet B

Stitches

Bullion stitch
Detached chain stitch
Fly stitch
French knot
Stem stitch
Straight stitch

Materials

- Nightdress
- DMC stranded cotton in white
- DMC Flower Thread in white
- DMC Coton Perlé no. 12 in white
- Rajmahal Art Silk in white
- Crewel needle size 9
- Straw needle size 8
- Tracing paper
- Black pen and HB pencil

◄ These beautiful embroidered flowers can be arranged to fit around the neckline of any nightgown. Worked with bullion stitch and other embroidery stitches, the effect is simple to achieve.

METHOD

1 Copy the neckline of your nightgown onto tracing paper with the black pen. Add the design (see fold-out sheet B), adjusting it to fit your nightgown. Using the pencil, transfer the design to the nightgown.

2 Start the embroidery with the rose sprays. To make the bullion roses, use two threads of stranded cotton and the straw needle. Work two bullion stitches of five twists side by side for the centre and five of eleven twists for the outside petals.

3 Work the stems in stem stitch, using one thread of flower thread and the crewel needle.

4 Using two threads of stranded cotton and the straw needle, stitch the rose buds, working two bullion stitches of seven twists side by side so that they touch at the top. Then with two threads of art silk and the crewel needle work straight stitch between the bullion stitches and fly stitch around the bud.

5 Add groups of five French knots to the sprays, using two threads of stranded cotton and the straw needle. Twist the thread twice around the needle.

6 Work the leaves in detached chain stitch, using two threads of art silk and the crewel needle. The rose sprays are now complete.

7 Work the five-petalled daisies in detached chain stitch with French knots at the centre. Use flower thread and the crewel needle.

8 Work the three-petalled daisies in the same way but using Coton Perlé.

Pansies and lace embroidered picture

The lace-like 'frame' of tiny mosaic stitches is in fact the main feature of this unusual picture.

In this gorgeous picture pansies worked in half cross stitch are surrounded by a frame worked primarily in eyelet and mosaic stitches using pearl cotton. The effect is of lace, continuing the old tradition of making embroidered (needlepoint) lace.

Finished size Embroidery 40 x 29.5 cm
Chart On fold-out sheet D

Stitches

French knot
Half cross stitch
Half eyelet stitch
Mosaic stitch
Rounded eyelet stitch
Smyrna cross
Straight stitch (beads)

➤ *Beautiful purple pansies in half cross stitch are the central element in this brilliant picture. The border consists of mosaic stitches, edged with eyelets and threaded with bead-studded ribbons.*

Mosaic infill

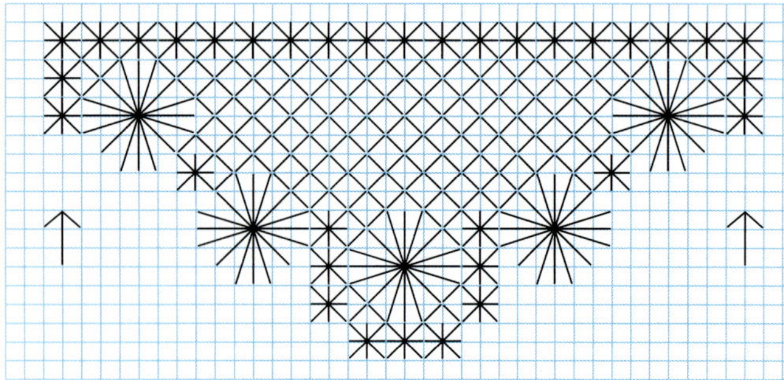

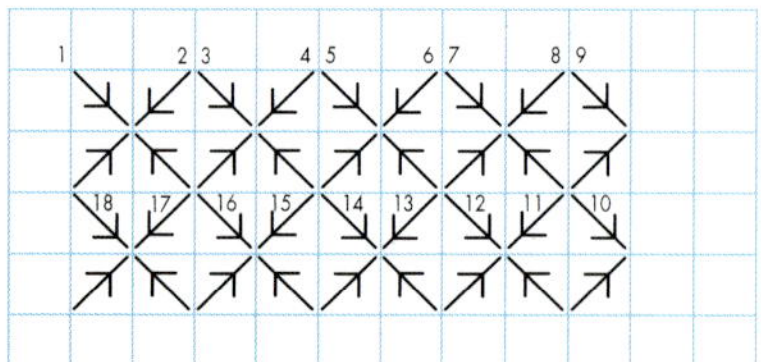

Stitch direction

Materials

- ◆ 60 x 50 cm piece of 18-count Aida in sage
- ◆ Coton Perlé no. 8 in ecru (3 balls)
- ◆ DMC stranded embroidery cotton in the following colours: medium green (320), light green (368), light pink (3354), deep pink (3733), medium blue-violet (340), light blue-violet (341), dark blue-violet (3746), topaz (727), dark brown (3371); ecru
- ◆ Tapestry needle size 26
- ◆ Straw needle size 10 (for beads)
- ◆ 4 m of 3 mm wide satin ribbon in chosen colour
- ◆ Mill Hill Glass Seed Beads in cream (00123)
- ◆ Embroidery frame

EMBROIDERY

1 Zigzag or overlock around the edge of the fabric. Place in embroidery frame. Measure 14 cm in from the side and base of the fabric and start the embroidery there (see the chart on fold-out sheet D).

2 Using the Coton Perlé and tapestry needle, embroider the four rows of the Smyrna cross framework, and the bars connecting the two inner rows, working each cross across two blocks (four threads) each way. The outer row consists of 329 x 93 Smyrna crosses (counting the corner ones both ways).

3 Beginning in the lower left-hand corner next to a Smyrna cross, work the rounded eyelets to make the inside scallop pattern. Stitch the eyelet from the centre out, placing a French knot (one twist) in the centre of each one.

4 Add the Smyrna crosses between the rounded eyelets to complete the inside scallops. Work the Smyrna crosses in the four vertical dividers. Add the half-eyelet stitches on either side of the dividers.

5 Embroider the outside scallop pattern in the same way as the inside one.

6 Using four strands of embroidery cotton, work the rows of pansies in half cross stitch across one square (two threads), according to the key on the fold-out sheet. There are three rows of pansies with blue border and two rows of pansies and tiny pink flowers with green border (see the photograph).

7 Fill the scallop patterns with mosaic stitch (see the diagram above). Follow the diagram carefully and do not turn the work during this embroidery or the sides will look different.

ADDING THE RIBBON

1 Measure enough ribbon to cover all four sides of the work plus an extra 20 cm. Widen the fabric hole at one corner and pull one end of the ribbon through. Leave a 6 mm tail.

2 With the straw needle and two strands of ecru embroidery cotton, use straight stitches to attach the glass beads according to the chart. When you reach the corner, fold the ribbon in a right angle in the opposite direction to which it is going and then back in the correct direction. Put a stitch in the loop formed by the ribbon to hold it in position. Then continue around the frame, attaching the glass beads as you go. When you reach your starting point, come across the ribbon, widen the starting hole and take the ribbon through to the back. Slip stitch both ends in place. Repeat for the second ribbon frame.

TO FINISH

Place the finished work face down on a soft towel and steam it gently. Block it into shape if necessary.

LACE

Lace is made by twisting and knotting threads rather than working on fabric. Needlepoint lace, made with needle and thread, was probably first made in Italy in the fifteenth century, bobbin lace, made by weaving threads wound around bobbins, in Flanders in the sixteenth century.

SAMPLERS AND PICTURES

A sampler is an embroidered panel on linen worked in various stitches. They are now made most often to commemorate a special event, such as a birth or a wedding, and they may include the alphabet and each number as well as appropriate motifs.

Samplers first appeared in the sixteenth century. Before that most elaborate embroidery had been produced in professional workshops but from this time embroidery became more a pursuit of individuals. They copied stitches from wherever they could, and in order not to forget them, stitched them onto a piece of fabric which became a reference tool (the word 'sampler' comes from the French *essamplaire*, meaning 'something copied or imitated'). These fabric records were usually narrow but could be very long and they were greatly valued—some were mentioned in wills and Royal inventories of the period. It was in response to this same demand for new stitches that the first pattern book was printed in 1523, by Johann Sibmacher in Augsburg in Germany. Later others were produced in Italy, France and England but they were rare and samplers remained the main method of recording embroidery stitches and patterns. The earliest European sampler with a fixed provenance is dated to 1598. It shows different motifs arranged in a random fashion on a piece of linen.

By the seventeenth century many more stitches were being used in embroidery and pattern books were more common. Samplers continued to be made as records, but they now acquired a new function, as exercises produced when young girls were learning to embroider. Most were stitched on linen or silk, and cross and tent stitches predominated, although other stitches such as cutwork and eyelets could be added for variety. As part of their new function, many now included an alphabet and, from the middle of the century on, also numerals—these were important as initials and dates were used for marking linen and so were essential to the girls' future housewifely duties. Animals, fruit and flowers were popular motifs on these samplers, and human figures and houses also appeared.

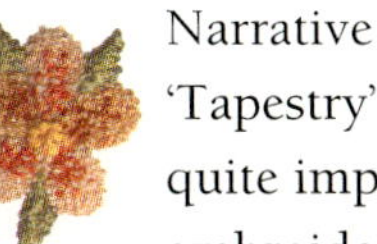

Narrative hangings such as the Bayeaux 'Tapestry' (in effect an embroidery) were a quite important element of medieval embroidery and pictorial elements had been present in some earlier embroidered works, in particular in panels on Elizabethan cushions. However, it was only during the seventeenth century that the concept of an embroidered picture, a definitive composition in itself, took hold. Small pictures, usually showing Biblical or mythological scenes, were embroidered mainly in canvas work or stumpwork. They were framed, set behind glass and hung on the wall.

By the eighteenth century samplers had lost their function as a reference tool and become solely a practical exercise, mostly worked in cross stitch. They were now usually square and the arrangement of motifs could be more complicated, sometimes with a central symmetrical design and a floral or geometric border around the edge. They were often used to record births, deaths or marriages and could include a family tree with names and dates. Some contained a pictorial element and Biblical scenes (especially Adam and Eve, and the return of the spies from Canaan) were especially popular. It was at this time that sampler working reached its peak.

In the nineteenth century the standard of samplers declined. Common types were those with a house in the centre, or groups of different motifs could be stitched, the whole held together by a border. Also popular were samplers with a pious verse or text. Linen was still used for some samplers but woollen canvas was now common. This century was also characterised by Berlin woolwork samplers, which often showed elaborate compositions, but samplers did become more standardised and rigid in style.

The tradition of embroidered pictures had continued through the eighteenth and nineteenth centuries, showing increasing naturalism and a preference for flower arrangements, although the range of subjects expanded greatly and included landscapes, animals and family groups.

Richelieu traycloth

The Richelieu buttonhole bars are used in the flower design worked in one corner of the traycloth.

Richelieu cutwork is a form of delicate openwork characterised by buttonhole bars that cross the cut areas. Here it is used on a lovely traycloth.

Finished size 40 x 30 cm
Embroidery motif On fold-out sheet A

Stitches

Buttonhole stitch
Buttonholed eyelet stitch
Double buttonhole stitch
Running stitch
Satin stitch
Stem stitch
Straight stitch

Materials

- 50 x 40 cm of white linen fabric
- DMC stranded embroidery cotton in white (2 skeins)
- Crewel needle size 9
- HB pencil
- 50 x 40 cm sheet of tracing paper
- Black pen
- Cellotape
- Small, pointed embroidery scissors

TRACING THE PATTERN

1 Pull a single thread along the edge of the material to use as a straight grain line.
2 Trace the pattern on fold-out sheet A onto tracing paper using the black pen. Tape the paper pattern to a clean window or light box and place the material over the pattern, making sure the straight grain line is parallel with the pattern edge and approximately 2 cm above the top of the pattern. Tape it in place. Using the pencil and starting with the corner motif, trace the pattern onto the fabric. Continue the scallops around the edges.

EMBROIDERY

1 Begin with the buttonhole bars. They are attached to the cloth at either end (points A and B in the diagram below) but are otherwise free of the fabric. Bring up the thread at the left-hand side (A), then make a small stitch at the right-hand side (B), and then one at A again. Work buttonhole stitches over these bars, taking care that the stitches do not enter the material except for one or two stitches at each end to anchor the bars so that they don't pull away when the background is cut. When all the embroidery is completed, the material will be cut away from both sides leaving just a buttonholed 'bridge', but don't be tempted to cut anything until the embroidery is completed because handling may cause the edges to look rubbed.
2 When the buttonhole bars are completed, take two strands of thread and run a line of small running stitches along between the pattern lines for the double buttonhole stitch so that it will have a slightly raised

Richelieu bar

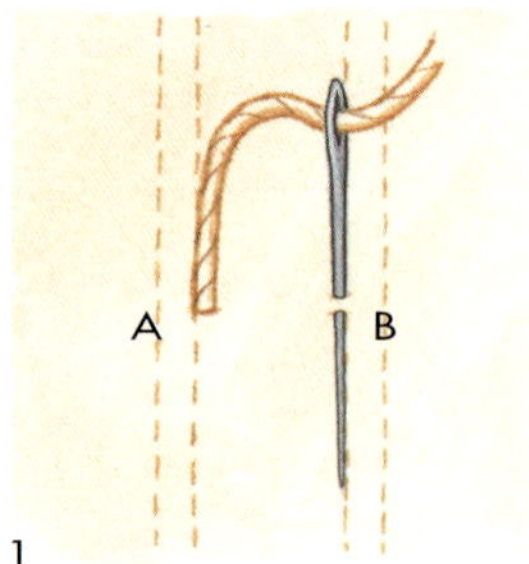

1

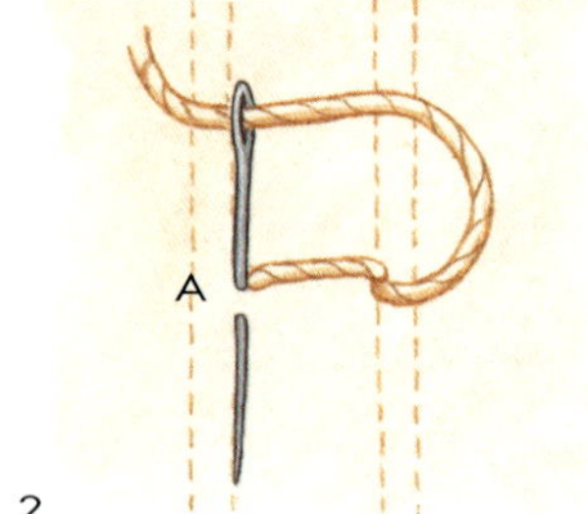

2

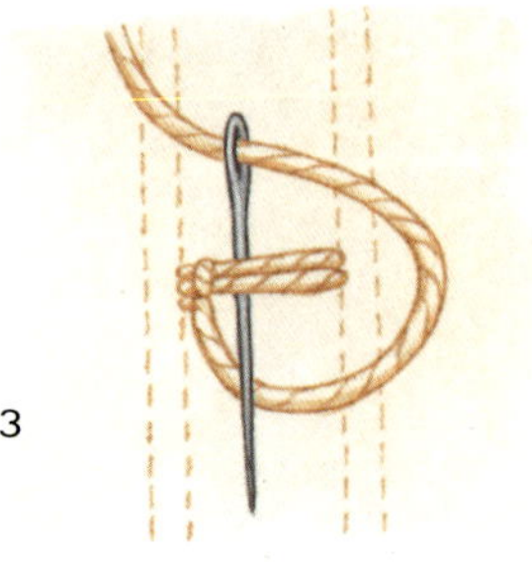

3

Worked primarily in buttonhole and double buttonhole stitches, this traycloth has a delicate cutwork pattern in one corner and is finished with a dainty scalloped edge. It would look equally at home as a placemat.

effect. Take a single thread and work the double buttonhole stitch along the lines indicated. To do this, work a row of buttonhole stitches with the loops along one edge of the pattern line, spacing the stitches one thread's width apart. Then work another row from the opposite direction, stitching between the original stitches, just inside the looped edge.

3 Work buttonhole stitching around the edges of the flower and leaves, using two strands of thread, and making sure the loops lie along the edges that will be cut. Still using two strands of thread, work the leaf veins and the stems of the sprays in stem stitch and the buds on the sprays in satin stitch. The centre of the flower is worked in buttonholed eyelet stitch and straight stitch.

4 Finally, work the scalloped edge with buttonhole stitch, padding it with running stitch as before or with small chain stitches.

TO FINISH

1 When all stitching is complete, spray the fabric with a good pre-wash stain remover and rinse, first in warm, sudsy water and then in clear, cold water. If pencil marks are still visible, soak the cloth for about 15 minutes in bleach and rinse thoroughly. Dry it in the sun only until it is dry enough to iron, and then iron it dry on the wrong side.

2 Using a pair of small, sharp, pointed embroidery scissors cut away the material below the 'bridges' according to the pattern.

Ribbon rose handkerchief sachet

This elegant damask sachet is lined with satin, while matching handmade cord provides a neat edging. It will be a real joy to fold away your special handkerchiefs in this sachet, or you could even use it as an evening bag.

Ribbon embroidery is currently enjoying a revival in popularity and its associations with later nineteenth century bric-a-brac should give it a place in any heirloom collection.

Finished size 20 x 19 cm
Embroidery design On fold-out sheet C

Stitches

Detached chain stitch
Fly stitch
Raised stem stitch
Silk ribbon embroidery (roses, leaves, loop stitch, straight stitch, detached twisted chain stitch)

Materials

- 55 x 26 cm of off-white damask
- 52 x 22 cm of off-white satin lining
- 1 m of 10 mm wide Terra Rosa bias overdyed silk ribbon in moss
- 2 m of 7 mm wide YLI pure silk ribbon in off-white (1)
- 2 m of 4 mm wide YLI pure silk ribbon in off-white (1)
- 50 cm of 7 mm wide YLI pure silk ribbon in pale green (31)
- 50 cm of 4 mm wide YLI pure silk ribbon in pale green (31)
- Soie d'Alger thread in cream
- Kacoonda fine silk thread no. 8 in pale green
- Kacoonda medium overdyed silk thread no. 8E
- Machine thread
- 1 packet Mill Hill Antique Glass Beads (03021)
- Crewel needle size 8
- Tapestry needle size 26
- Straw needle size 3
- Chenille needle size 22
- 20 cm embroidery hoop
- Fine tip water-soluble pen
- Black pen
- Brown paper
- Tracing paper

Pattern for sachet

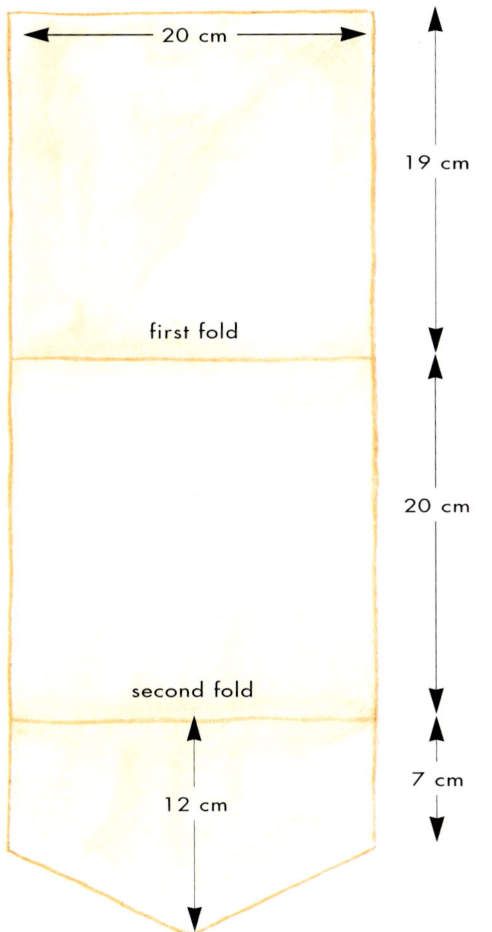

PREPARATION

1 Following the diagram at left and using the brown paper, make a paper pattern for the sachet.
2 Pin the pattern to the damask and tack around the edges and along the two fold lines. Place the paper so that there is room around the flap for the embroidery hoop. Remove the paper.
3 Trace the embroidery design on fold-out sheet C onto tracing paper, using the black pen. Tape the tracing to a window or light box and position the fabric flap over the design with the right side facing you. Tape it in place and use the water-soluble pen to

A single ribbon rose is stitched to the back of the sachet.

Making a ribbon rose

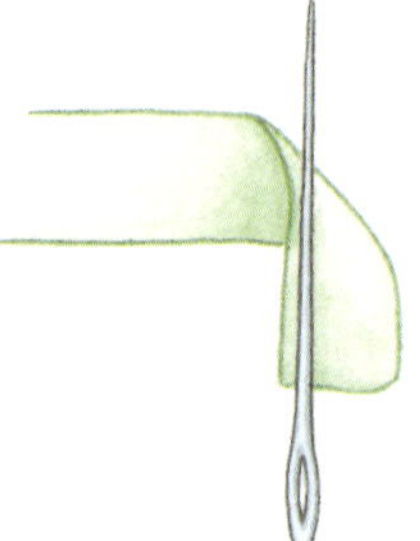

1 Fold down one end of the green ribbon and lay the straw needle on it.

2 Roll the ribbon around the needle.

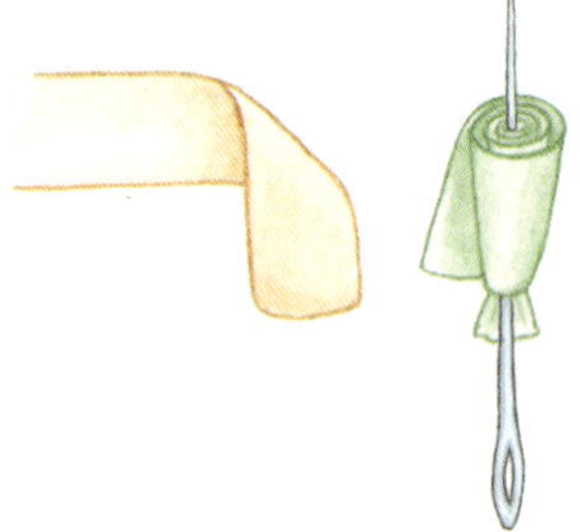

3 Stitch through base of rolled ribbon. Fold down one end of the off-white ribbon.

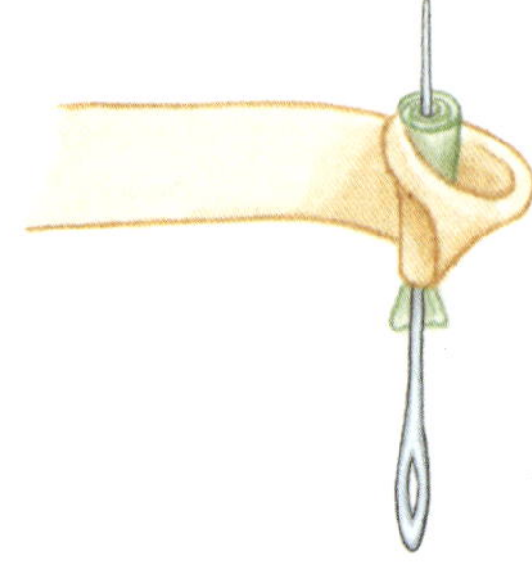

4 Stitch folded end of the off-white ribbon to the green ribbon and roll.

transfer the design to the fabric. Trace off the outline of the thick stems. Mark the centre of the full roses and blossoms with a dot. Draw a straight line for the rose buds and small leaves. Remove the fabric and place it in the embroidery hoop.

EMBROIDERY

1 Work the raised stem stitch using two strands of the Soie D'Alger cream silk thread in the crewel needle. Begin with the bars, spacing them 3 mm apart. Thread the tapestry needle with one strand of the same thread and work the stem stitch evenly over the bars so that the rows of stitches touch each other.
2 Make six silk ribbon roses, five for the flap and one for the back of the sachet (see the diagram at left). Cut the 7 mm wide pale green silk ribbon into six 8 cm lengths. Thread the crewel needle with sewing thread and lay aside. Fold one end of a length of ribbon over on an angle and lay the straw needle over the fold. Roll the ribbon around the needle a few times and then use the crewel needle and thread to

Ribbon roses and blossoms are massed together on the flap of this beautiful handkerchief sachet. The subtle cream and pale green colouring of the ribbons ensures the embroidery enhances but does not overwhelm the damask.

stitch through the base of the rose. Roll the remaining silk ribbon around the needle, fold the end over and stitch through the base several times. Take the 7 mm wide off-white silk ribbon, fold down one end and stitch it to the base of the green ribbon. Keep folding, winding in the same direction and stitch each time until the rose is the desired size. Secure it well at the base and remove the crewel needle but leave the thread attached. Remove the straw needle. Repeat to make five more roses.

3 To make the rose leaves, cut thirteen 3.5 cm lengths from the Terra Rosa silk ribbon. Take one piece, fold both ends into the centre to make a point. Run a gathering thread across the lower edge, pull the thread and secure it. Leave the thread attached. Trim the cut ends of the ribbon. Make the remaining leaves.

Rose leaves

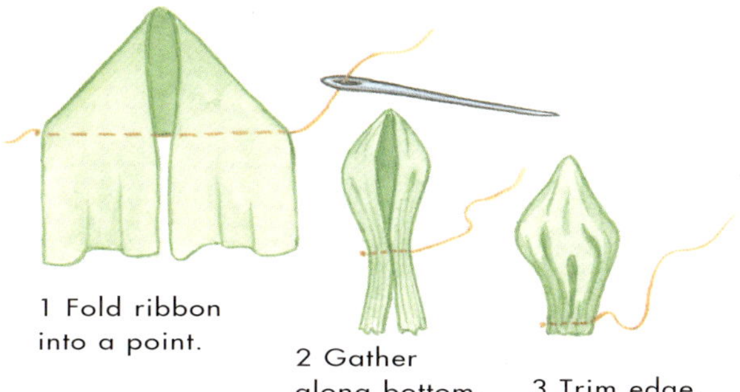

4 Sew the leaves in position on the flap and sew two leaves in the centre of the back. Sew the roses on top of the leaves.

5 To make the five-petalled blossoms, first attach three beads securely to the centre of the flower. Using the 4 mm wide off-white ribbon and the chenille needle, work five loop stitches closely around the beads. Come up in the centre of the flower and go down 3 mm out. Avoid pulling the last petal out of shape as you stitch the next one. Use the fine green silk thread to embroider two straight stitches from the centre of each petal.

Loop stitch

6 For the three-petalled flowers attach two beads securely to the centre. Work as for the five-petalled flowers but use only three loop stitches.

7 To make the rose buds, use the 4 mm wide pale green silk ribbon and work a padded straight stitch for the centre. With the 4 mm wide off-white ribbon make a twisted chain stitch either side of the green centre. Take the Terra Rosa ribbon and use it to form the sepals by working a single straight stitch either side of the bud. With the medium green silk thread embroider a fly stitch over the Terra Rosa ribbon and add one straight stitch in the middle. With fine green silk thread work a fly stitch on the tip of the bud.

Padded straight stitch

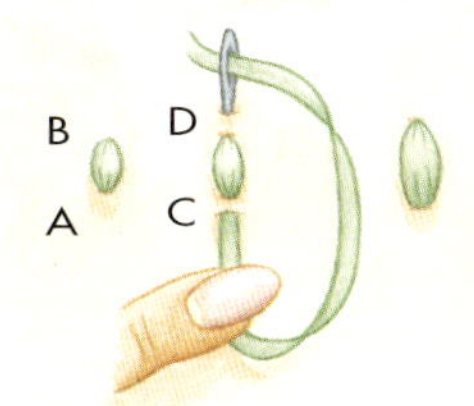

Detached twisted chain stitch

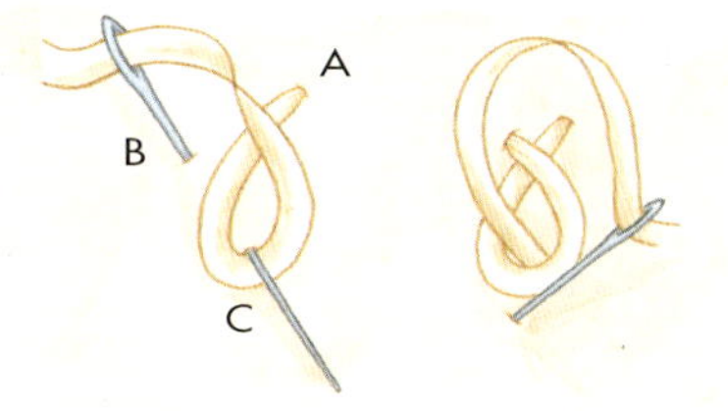

8 The small leaves are worked in the medium green silk thread using detached chain stitch. Leave a longer catching stitch at the tip. Work the small leaves on the flap and a couple on the back.

ASSEMBLING THE SACHET

1 Remove the embroidery from the hoop. Trim around the sachet leaving a 1 cm seam allowance.

2 Cut out a matching piece from the satin lining.

3 Place right sides of damask and lining together; machine stitch around the edges, using 1 cm seams. Leave an opening in the end. Turn through; press.

4 Sew the opening closed. Fold the sachet on the first fold and slip stitch the sides of the sachet together.

TO FINISH

1 Make a twisted cord from the Soie D'Alger thread. Cut fifteen 2.4 m lengths of thread and knot both ends. Attach one end to a hook or door knob. Slip a pencil in the other end and twist it until the cord starts to twist back on itself. Remove the pencil, fold the cord in half and allow it to twist.

2 Sew the cord along both sides of the sachet and around the flap.

ABCDEFGHIJKLM
NOPQRSTUVWXYZ
0123456789
15-3 TASMAN 1995
M R

Tree of life cross-stitch birth sampler

The parents' initials are placed on either side of the tree of life.

Celebrate the birth of a treasured baby with this lovely sampler, which incorporates many traditional European symbols of birth and fertility, including a cradle, storks and tree of life.

Finished size Embroidered panel 38 x 25.5 cm
Chart On fold-out sheet E

Stitches

Algerian eyelet stitch
Back stitch
Cross stitch

Materials

- ◆ 63 x 50 cm of white linen, 10 fabric threads per 1 cm
- ◆ DMC stranded embroidery cottons in the colours and quantities in the colour key
- ◆ Tapestry needle size 24 or 26

METHOD

1 Work large overcast stitches around the edge of the linen to stop it fraying.
2 Measure in about 12.5 cm from the right-hand lower corner and begin working the outer frame. The chart is on fold-out sheet E. Each symbol represents one cross stitch worked over two fabric threads, using two strands of cotton. Work all the cross stitch first.
3 Using one strand of light antique blue (932) fill in the backgrounds of the stork panels and the top of the cradle panel, above the green 'branch'.
4 Work the panels of Algerian eyelets using one strand of medium burnished gold (3821) and working each eyelet over four fabric threads. For the panel below the alphabet first work two rows of back stitch, working each stitch over two fabric threads, and then three rows of eyelets, placed so that they are staggered. Work the panels below the date of birth in the same way but use only two rows of eyelets.
5 Use back stitch or straight stitch to work outlines, using one strand of cotton over two fabric threads.
■ *Flower motifs below birds, beside row of numbers.* Outline flowers in medium shell pink (223), and then outline leaves and work details in the medium green-grey (3052).
■ *Border below row of numbers and above stork and cradle panels.* Outline hearts in medium shell pink (223), and outline green-grey areas and work details in medium green-grey (3052).
■ *Blue and yellow border beside top of tree.* Outline in medium antique blue (931).
■ *Tree.* Outline the light shell pink stars in medium shell pink (223), the light green stars in medium green-grey (3052) and the blue star in medium antique blue (931), and work details in medium green-grey (3052).
■ *Base of tree.* Outline the two shell pink flowers in medium shell pink (223) and work details of base in medium antique blue (931).
■ *Crowns above parents' initials.* Work the three straight stitches at base of crown in medium burnished gold (3821) using two strands of cotton.

TO FINISH

1 Stretch and frame as desired.
2 Write the name of the maker and date of completion on the back of the framed sampler. You can also record there additional information, such as the surname.

◄ Worked in cross stitch with Algerian eyelet stitches for variety, this sampler is the perfect way to commemorate a baby's birth. Select the letters you need from the complete alphabet provided.

Blossom cross-stitched cushion

Worked mostly in cross stitch on Aida, this lovely cushion is easy to stitch, even for a beginner.

The delicate colours of this flannel flower and gum blossom design make an unusual and very lovely cushion. It looks beautifully fresh and modern but will quickly become a family heirloom.

Finished size Cushion 40 x 40 cm; embroidery 28 x 28 cm
Chart On fold-out sheet E

Stitches

Cross stitch
French knot
Straight stitch

Materials

- Two pieces of white 18-count Aida evenweave fabric, 46 x 46 cm
- Machine thread in white
- DMC stranded embroidery cottons in the colours in the colour key, plus cranberry (605) and dusty rose (963)
- Tapestry needle size 26
- 40 cm cushion insert

METHOD

1 Find the centre of one square of fabric and divide the fabric into quarters, marking the lines with running stitches. Work the flower design in cross stitch following the chart on fold-out sheet E, using two strands of cotton over one fabric square. Add the French knots as indicated in topaz (726). The stamens of the gum blossom are worked in straight stitches using one strand each of cranberry (605) and dusty rose (963). The chart gives one-quarter of the design. Each quarter is a mirror image of the adjoining quarter (see the photograph).

2 When the flower design is completed, work the border. The outside row should be 206 stitches on each side.

3 To make up the cushion, place the two squares of fabric with right sides together and machine around the edges, leaving a plain area 6 cm wide around the outside of the cross stitch. The cushion will be 40 cm square. Leave an opening to insert the cusion.

4 Turn right side out and insert the cushion. Slip stitch the opening closed.

➤ *Bright pink gum blossoms make a lovely contrast to the more subtle greens and whites on this cushion. The blossoms are worked in straight stitches and French knots for further contrast.*

Cross stitch

Cross stitch is one of the most popular of embroidery stitches. It has a very long history in the embroidery of Europe and early examples have been identified from the areas of Iran and India. Cross stitch can be worked on any fabric but is usually worked on canvas, linen or other evenweave fabric. Gingham is also used as its squares form a natural grid. Cross stitch is one of the stitches traditionally used on needlepoint. There are many variations. It can be worked in a design that contrasts with the unworked background or it can completely cover the base cloth. In Assisi embroidery the design is left unworked and stitches fill the background.

Pansy tablecloth

The petals of these pansies are worked in long and short stitch for good coverage, while the leaves and ribbons are in satin stitch.

This charming cloth—it has a bunch of pansies in each corner—will find many uses. Traditionally tablecloths such as this were often called afternoon tea cloths, and they were an essential part of the embroidery women stitched for their 'boxes', in preparation for marriage.

Finished size 93 x 93 cm
Embroidery motif On fold-out sheet B

Stitches

Long and short stitch
Satin stitch
Stem stitch
Straight stitch

Materials

- 1 m square of tablecloth linen.
- DMC stranded embroidery cottons in the following colours: dark yellow (726), light yellow (745), blue-violet (340), apricot (722), brown (838), light blue (828)
- Overdyed silk in green variegated (133)
- Caron Waterlilies overdyed thread in lemon meringue, amethyst, prairie fire
- Crewel needle size 7/9
- Tracing paper
- Black pen
- Sharp lead pencil
- Machine thread to match linen
- Embroidery hoop

◄ Pansies are always popular and the beautiful variegated threads used on this cloth ensure no two flowers are exactly the same. The motif could be used just as effectively on a round cloth, if that suits your setting better.

EMBROIDERY

1 Turn a 1 cm hem around all sides of the linen.
2 Using the pen, trace the design on fold-out sheet B onto tracing paper and tape it to a window or light box. Tape the linen over it and, using the pencil, trace the design onto the linen. Place a motif in each corner, at least 8 cm in from the corner.
3 Using the embroidery hoop and two strands of thread, work the embroidery one corner at a time. Embroider the pansy petals in long and short stitch, working the edges in variegated colour and the inner part in plain colour. For the small pansy use lemon meringue variegated silk and dark yellow (726), for the medium pansy use amethyst variegated silk and blue-violet (340), and for the large pansy use prairie fire variegated silk and apricot (722).
4 Embroider the centres in straight stitch, using one strand of light yellow (745) stranded cotton, with one strand of brown (838) for the markings.
5 Using two strands of green variegated silk; work the leaves in satin stitch and the stems in stem stitch.
6 Work the ribbons in satin stitch using two strands of light blue stranded cotton.

TO FINISH

1 When all the embroidery is completed, turn in a 2.5 cm hem around the cloth and use matching thread to hem around it. The corners may be left square or mitred.
2 Press with a steam iron on the wrong side.

Bee and flower knot brooches

Whether you prefer a classic flower design or an interesting little bee, these brooches will add a cachet to any outfit. They also provide the perfect opportunity to become expert at two different knot stitches.

These two elegant little brooches are worked entirely in knot stitches, French knots for the whimsical bee and colonial knots for the more traditional flower.

FLOWER BROOCH

Finished size Motif 4 x 2.5 cm

Stitch

Colonial knot

Materials

- ◆ 18 x 18 cm of silk fabric
- ◆ 18 x 18 cm of muslin
- ◆ DMC stranded embroidery cotton in the following colours: salmon (760), light salmon (761), terracotta (758), light pink (225), khaki green (3012), fern green (523), orange (402), yellow (726)
- ◆ Crewel embroidery needle size 9
- ◆ 4 inch embroidery hoop
- ◆ Sharp, hard pencil
- ◆ Tracing paper
- ◆ Brooch frame

Method

1 Trace the design below onto tracing paper. Tape it to a window or light box and tape the silk over it. Using the sharp pencil, transfer the outline to the silk.

Flower motif

2 Baste the silk and muslin together (you embroider through both). Place it into the hoop.

3 Using one strand of cotton and colonial knots, fill each outlined area, working the light colour first and

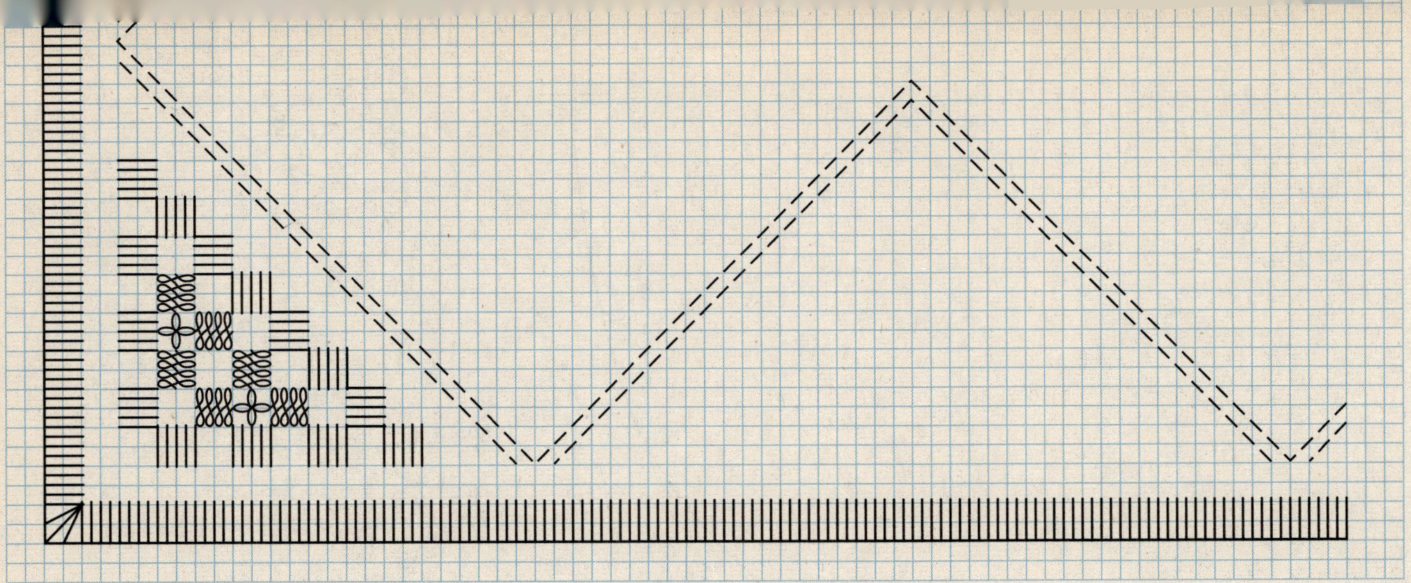

WOOL EMBROIDERED BLANKET

grass

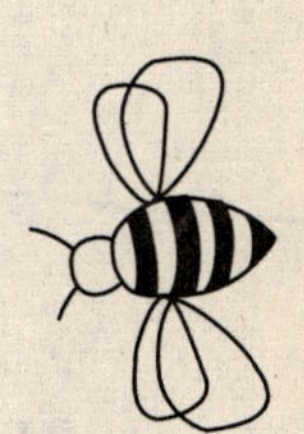

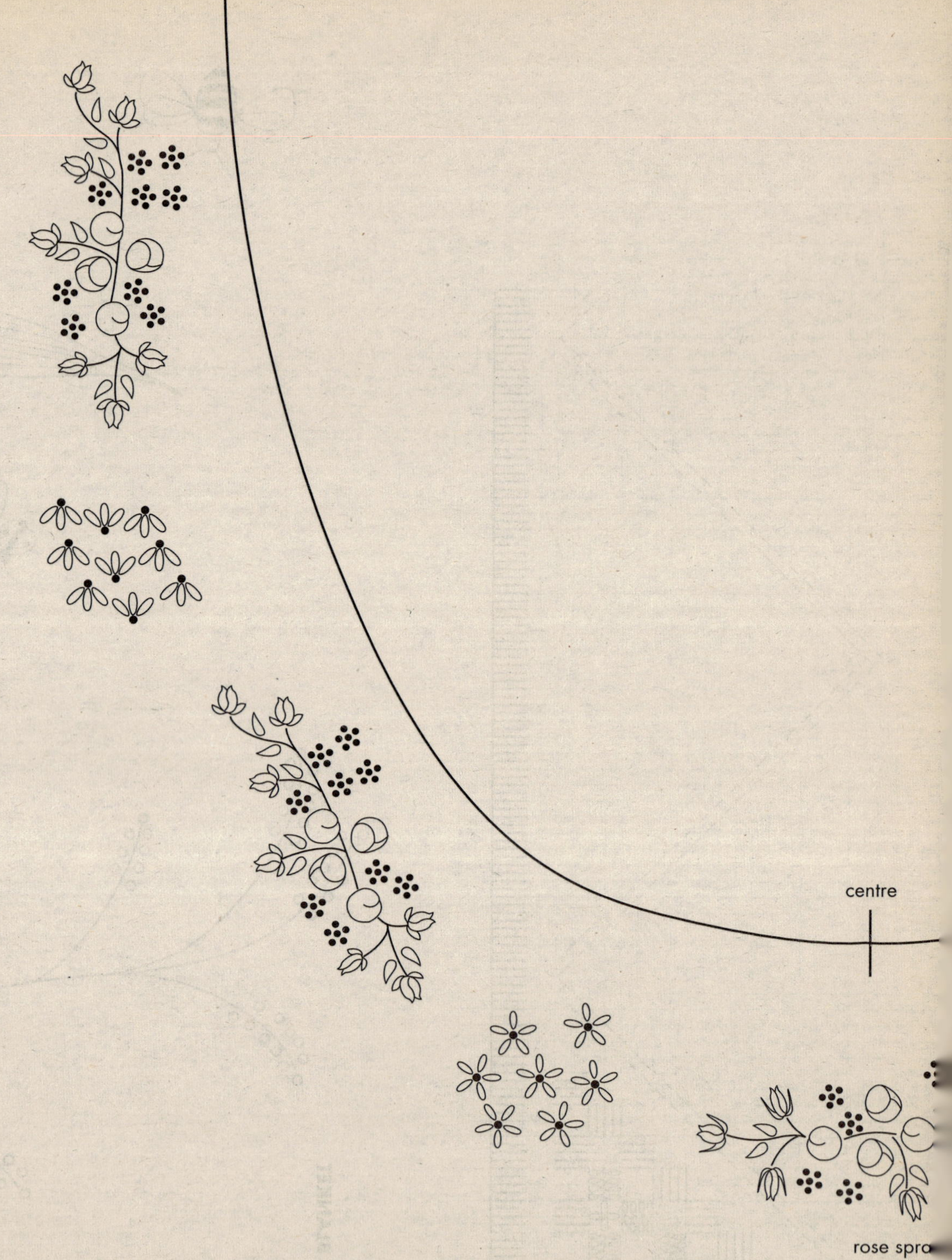
centre
rose spra

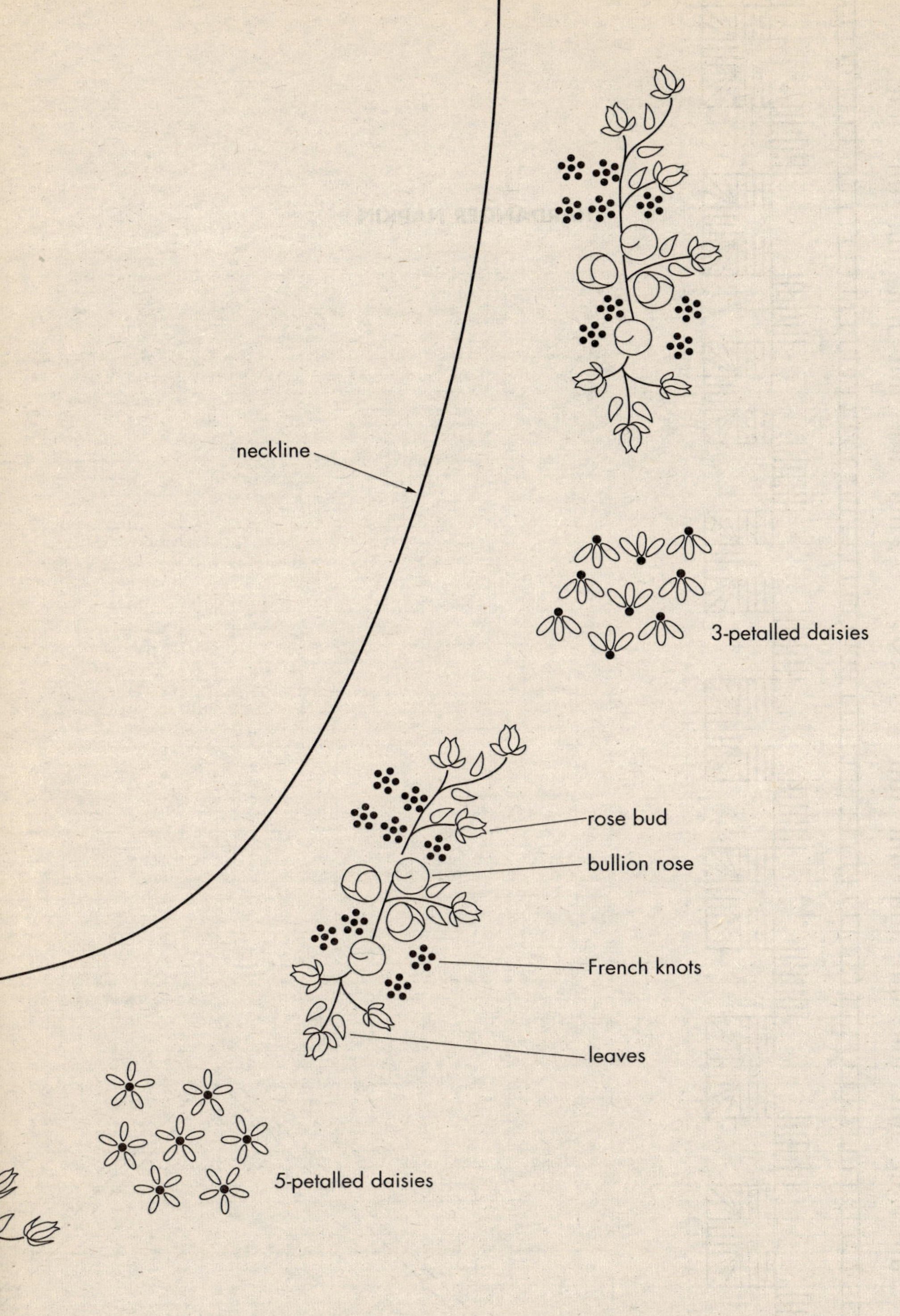
neckline
3-petalled daisies
rose bud
bullion rose
French knots
leaves
5-petalled daisies

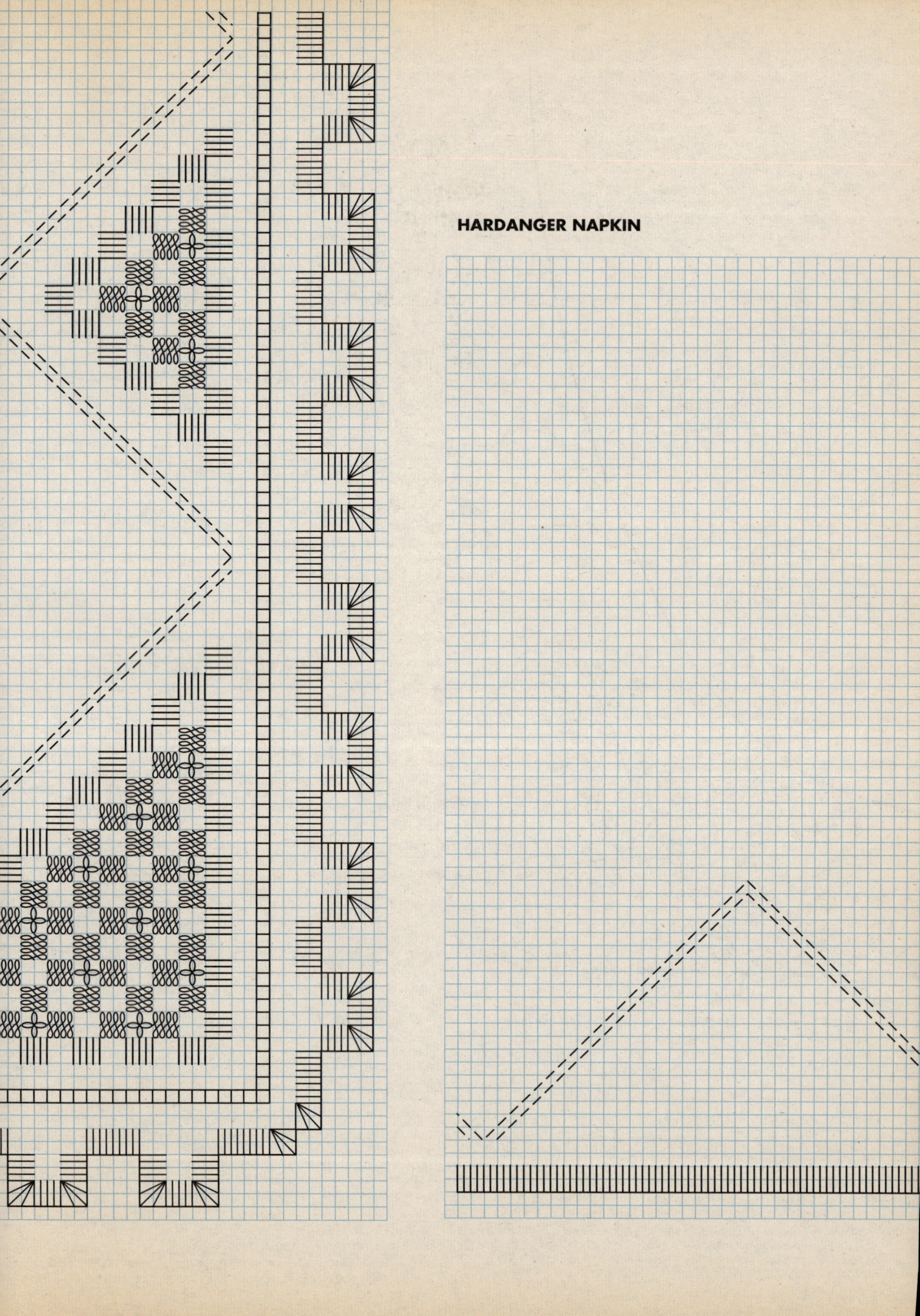
HARDANGER NAPKIN

then the dark colour over the light. Fill the top petal and the two bottom ones with light salmon (761) and add salmon (760) towards the centre. For the other two petals use light pink (225) and terracotta (758). Use fern green (523) down the centre of each leaf with khaki green (3012) on either side. Work the centre in yellow (726), with orange (402) knots scattered across it.

4 Remove the embroidery from the hoop and press it on the wrong side, avoiding the embroidered area. Frame according to the maker's instructions.

Knot stitches have many functions in embroidery. They can be used individually to provide a point of emphasis, such as an eye or flower centre, or massed to give texture, as here.

BEE BROOCH

Finished size Bee approximately 3 x 3 cm

Stitches

French knot

Straight stitch

Materials

- ◆ 18 x 18 cm of silk fabric
- ◆ 18 x 18 cm of muslin
- ◆ DMC stranded embroidery cotton in the following colours: beige (739), peach (3770), yellow (742), brown (3371), light blue-green (504)
- ◆ Tiny black bead
- ◆ Crewel embroidery needle size 9
- ◆ 4 inch embroidery hoop
- ◆ Sharp, hard pencil
- ◆ Brooch frame

Method

1 Trace the design below and work the embroidery as for the flower, but use one strand of thread and French knots of one twist to fill each outlined area.

2 Using light blue-green (504), fill the background with knots, covering enough area to fill your chosen frame and a little beyond.

3 Using brown thread and straight stitches, add the legs and antennae with a French knot at the end of each antenna.

4 Sew on the bead to indicate the eye.

5 Remove the embroidery from the hoop and press it on the wrong side, avoiding the embroidered area. Frame according to the maker's instructions.

Beadwork

Beadwork is a very old form of embroidery, and rows of beads that had been sewn to garments were found in burials from about 20,000 BC. Seed pearls and other beads were used extensively on elaborate medieval church embroideries, and they were stitched to the heavily embroidered clothing of the Tudor and Stuart periods. In the following centuries there was a vogue for small pictures and panels made entirely of tiny, coloured glass beads in vivid colours, and the use of beaded motifs to give emphasis and relief to embroidered pictures continues to this day. Using beadwork to cover small bags is another very old tradition continued in modern evening bags.

White iris evening bag

Seed pearls are stitched to the bag for an extra touch of luxury.

An iris rising from a bed of roses and daisies provides the design on this beautiful evening bag, which is stitched in white and cream and finished with seed pearls to make a bag worthy of a Victorian duchess.

Finished size Height 24 cm; diameter 14 cm
Embroidery motif On fold-out sheet F

Stitches

Bullion stitch
Buttonhole stitch
Colonial knot
Detached chain stitch
Fly stitch
Long and short stitch
Pistil stitch
Satin stitch
Stem stitch
Straight stitch

➤ *This embroidered silk reticule is the perfect accessory for a formal evening dress, whether you're attending a night at the opera, a ball or even a very fancy dinner. And it's large enough to hold all those essential bits and pieces.*

An elegant iris worked in long and short stitch forms the central feature of this embroidery design. The white and off-white threads, in a range of thicknesses and finishes, and the tiny seed pearls provide subtle but effective contrast against the silk.

White work

Any form of white-on-white embroidery is known as white work, and most forms now in use developed as copies of lace costume accessories. These are some of the more common forms.

■ Danish white work is worked in linen or cotton thread on fine lawn.

■ Hedebo and Amager white work is characterised by a combination of floral decoration and drawn thread work.

■ Ayrshire embroidery is a Scottish 'sewed muslin' white work that used cotton threads on muslin. It originated in the Edinburgh area and had become an important industry by the end of the eighteenth century. It often imitated French lace, which was difficult to obtain in Britain during the Napoleonic wars. Ayrshire embroidery is sewn with a hook instead of a needle.

■ Guipure work involved darning on net to imitate sixteenth century lace. It became fashionable in the nineteenth century.

■ In the nineteenth century white work was encouraged in Ireland to provide employment and utilise the cheap labour. The forms developed included Carrickmacross embroidery (an imitation lace) and Montmellick embroidery, which originated in the village of Montmellick.

Materials

- ◆ 40 cm of off-white silk
- ◆ 40 cm of off-white muslin
- ◆ 40 cm of off-white satin
- ◆ Off-white machine thread
- ◆ Tracing paper
- ◆ Black pen
- ◆ Sharp lead pencil
- ◆ Crewel needles sizes 7/9
- ◆ Embroidery hoop
- ◆ 2 m of white cord
- ◆ Two silver beads
- ◆ Seed pearls
- ◆ 1 m of 2 mm wide white silk ribbon
- ◆ 1 m of 4 mm wide cream silk ribbon
- ◆ DMC stranded embroidery cotton in white and off-white (746)
- ◆ Danish Flower Thread in off-white
- ◆ Soie d'Alger silk yarn in cream
- ◆ Madeira Decora thread in white (1471)
- ◆ Appleton crewel wool 991B

EMBROIDERY

1 From each of the silk, muslin and satin fabrics cut out a piece 34 x 26 cm and a 16.5 cm diameter circle.

2 Trace the design on fold-out sheet F onto tracing paper using the black pen. Tape it to a window or light box, tape the silk rectangle over it and use the pencil to trace the design onto the silk. We used the design twice (once reversed) but the bag would look equally effective worked only once at the centre of the front or even three times. Allow for seams when making up the bag.

3 Baste the muslin rectangle to the silk and zigzag stitch around the edges. Repeat with the muslin and silk circles.

4 Fit the hoop around the design area and work the design as follows.

A: Three leaves. Fly stitch in two strands of white DMC stranded cotton

B: Two buds. For each work three bullion stitches of eight twists in two strands of Soie d'Alger yarn

C: Two buds. Work two straight stitches between the bullion stitches using two strands of white DMC stranded cotton

D: Calyx. Fly stitch in two strands of white DMC stranded cotton

E: Iris. Colonial knots in one strand of DMC off-white (746) stranded cotton

F: Iris petals. Long and short stitch in one strand of Decora thread

G: Four leaves. Buttonhole stitch using the Danish Flower Thread

H: Daisy leaves. Detached chain stitch in 2 mm wide white silk ribbon

I: Grub roses. Work the centre satin stitches in crewel wool surrounded by two rows of bullion stitches of eight twists in two strands of Soie d'Alger yarn

J: Rose leaves. Detached chain stitch in 4 mm wide cream silk ribbon

K: Daisies. Five bullion stitches of ten twists in one strand of Decora thread

L: Daisy stems. Stem stitch in two strands of white DMC stranded cotton

M: Edging of lower iris petals and centre of top ones. Long and short stitch using two strands of Soie d'Alger yarn

N: Iris leaves. Satin stitch in two strands of white DMC stranded cotton

O: Stem. Stem stitch in two strands of white DMC stranded cotton

P: Pistil stitch in two strands of Decora thread

5 Attach three pearls to the centre of the iris, and then one to the centre of each daisy flower. Add rows of five or six pearls along the spine of each of the four large leaves. Scatter groups of three pearls at random across the fabric.

ASSEMBLING THE BAG

1 Place the right sides of the satin and silk rectangles together and stitch along the top edge (1 cm seam allowances have been allowed) and down the side to form a tube. Turn right side out.

2 Take tucks in bottom edge and fit onto silk circle. Machine stitch.

3 Turn under 1 cm on the satin circle and place it in the base of the bag to conceal the seams. Stitch it in place by hand.

4 Form a casing for the ties by machining two rows around the top of the bag through all layers. Place one row of stitching 3 cm down from the top edge and the second row 2 cm below that.

5 Make two buttonhole openings in the casing, one on either side of the bag. Cut the cord in half and thread it through the casing, one piece going in and out of one hole and the other piece going in and out of the other hole. Attach the silver beads to the ends of the ties and draw up the bag.

Shadow embroidered voile square

Unlike traditional shadow work, the embroidery on this voile square is stitched from the right side of the fabric, but it follows early styles in being white on white. It has a large floral design in the centre and a flower in each corner. The neat hem is finished with feather stitch.

Finished size 108 x 108 cm
Embroidery motifs On fold-out sheet C

Stitches

Double back stitch
Feather stitch
Satin stitch
Stem stitch

Materials

- 1.20 m of 115 cm wide voile
- Anchor stranded thread in white (1) (2 skeins)
- White machine thread
- Crewel needle size 9
- Tracing paper
- Fineline permanent marker pen
- Water-soluble marking pen or pencil, or sharp HB pencil
- Medium-sized embroidery hoop, if desired

PREPARATION

1 Using the permanent marker pen, trace the three designs on fold-out sheet C onto tracing paper.
2 Trim the fabric to an exact square, cutting off the selvedges and making sure all the cut edges are perfectly straight. Tack 15 mm double hems on all sides, mitring the corners. Using machine thread, feather stitch the hems with small, neat stitches.

➤ *You will find this lovely voile square has many uses. It can be thrown over a pram to protect baby from insects or glaring light, or used as a light summer shawl or bathtime wrap.*

A voile square is perfect as a throwover to keep insects off food and the embroidery makes it special enough to use when entertaining.

THE CENTRAL MOTIF

1 Find the exact centre of the fabric and tack lines through it horizontally and vertically. The lines should extend out at least 15 cm from the centre. Position the design for the centre motif under the centre of the fabric with the 'x' in the centre and pin it to prevent movement. Using the water-soluble pen or pencil, trace the design onto the fabric, making all lines as fine as possible. Remove the tacking lines from under this motif (but only as far as the outer petals—leave the rest of the tacking in place).

2 Pull two strands of embroidery cotton, about 45 cm long, separately from the skein and put them together. Thread the needle and work the design using double back stitch. Work from right to left. Insert the needle on the lower line of each petal, making two or three tiny running stitches toward the base of the petal. Take the needle through to the back of the work to the upper line, a few fabric threads to the left, and make a small back stitch. Bring the needle out on the lower line, again a few fabric threads to the left. Continue in this way making small back stitches on the right side of the fabric and closed herringbone stitches on the wrong side. Keep the stitches firm but not tight. Using an embroidery hoop is recommended. When working on a curved section of a petal, make smaller stitches on the inner curve and larger stitches on the outer curve. Finish each petal by running the thread through several herringbone stitches at the back of the work, close to the edge, and cut the thread. Do not carry the thread over to the next petal or leaf as it will show through. Keep the back of your work as neat as possible as it will be seen.

3 When the central design is completed, position the outer design in one quarter of the fabric, matching the dotted lines to the tacking. Pin, and trace off the stems and leaves only (tracing in small stages prevents the design being rubbed out). Embroider the stems using stem stitch and the leaves using satin stitch.

4 Reposition the design carefully, making sure the stems are in the correct place. Pin the design to the fabric and trace off the flowers. Embroider the petals in shadow stitch. Repeat the last two steps for the other three quarters of the outer design.

THE CORNER MOTIFS

Position the dotted lines of the corner design 5 cm in from the edge of the hem. Trace off the design and work the embroidery in the same way as for the central motif.

Satin and stem stitches are used to complement the shadow embroidery of the petals and complete the fresh floral design. Like the shadow work, they are worked on the right side of the fabric.

SHADOW WORK

Shadow work is embroidery that is worked on transparent or semi-transparent fabrics so that the threads show through from the wrong side to create a shadow effect. Originally the stitches were worked from the wrong side using crossed or double back stitch (or closed herringbone stitch), but it can also be worked from the right side of the fabric.

Shadow work was especially popular in the eighteenth century when it was used for white work. It is still a popular technique for white-on-white work but it is now often stitched with coloured threads. Surface embroidery stitches, in particular stem stitch and satin stitch, are often combined with the shadow work to indicate details of the design.

A number of other sewing techniques have also been adapted for use in shadow work, in particular quilting and appliqué. Shadow Italian quilting and trapunto quilting both lent themselves easily to shadow embroidery. In their shadow work equivalents, two layers of sheer fabric are tacked together and the outline of the design is embroidered through both. The outlined areas are then stuffed with brightly coloured wool to provide the coloured infill.

Shadow appliqué is a similar technique in which the required motifs are cut from coloured fabric and placed between two layers of sheer fabric. Running stitches are then worked around the edges of the coloured shapes to hold the three layers of fabric together.

Hardanger table setting

Norwegian Hardanger embroidery is one of the most effective forms of cutwork. Traditionally worked in white threads on white fabric, it is based on squared kloster blocks and needle woven bars, both of which are shown to advantage on this elegant placemat and napkin.

Finished size Cloth 40 x 32 cm; napkin 31 x 31 cm
Charts On fold-out sheet A

Stitches

Buttonhole stitch
Double back stitch
Four-sided stitch
Needle weaving
Satin stitch
Straight loop stitch

Materials

- 40 cm of 22-count hardanger with 9 double threads to 1 cm
- DMC Coton Perlé no. 8 in white (5200)
- DMC Coton Perlé no. 5 in white (5200)
- Tapestry needles sizes 24 and 26
- Sharp, fine-bladed scissors

THE PLACEMAT

1 Cut one piece of fabric measuring 50 x 40 cm for the placemat and one piece measuring 40 x 40 cm for the napkin. Zigzag or overlock around the edges. Mark the horizontal and vertical centre lines with tacking stitch.

2 Following the chart on fold-out sheet A (one square on the chart equals two blocks each way on the fabric), begin the kloster block embroidery in the left corner 8 cm in from each side. Kloster blocks are the basis of Hardanger embroidery and each block consists of five satin stitches worked over four

➤ *The repeated geometric patterns of Hardanger embroidery are ideally suited to a formal setting, as this placemat and napkin show. The patterns are further emphasised by the sheen of the pearl cotton against the matt fabric.*

threads. The blocks surround the cutwork area. The blocks may be worked from left to right or right to left, and the hole in each corner is shared with the next block. The kloster blocks on this project are worked in Coton Perlé no. 5, using tapestry needle size 26. The main design is worked on all four corners of the placemat, with two small triangle designs worked on each long side and one small triangle design worked on each short side.

Working kloster blocks

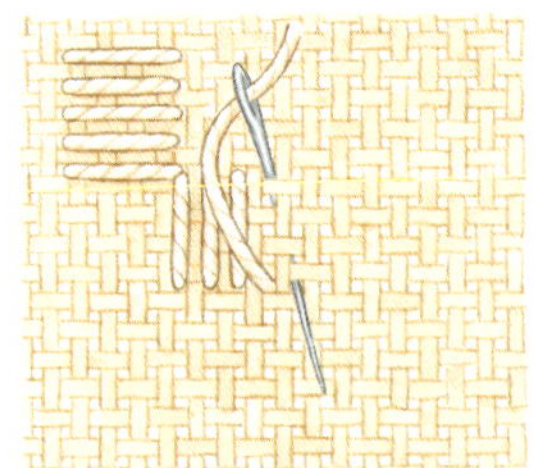

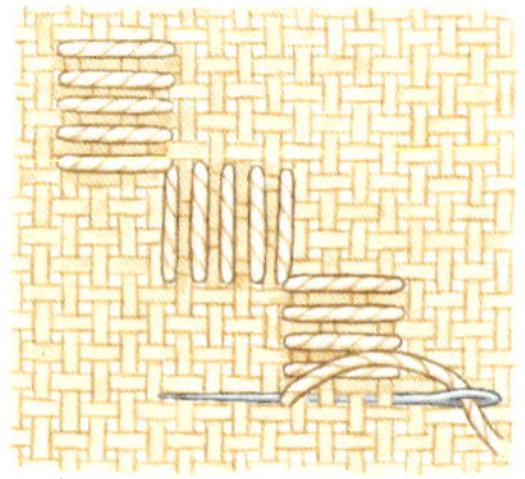

3 All the kloster blocks must be worked before you begin cutting the fabric. Always cut on the back of the work, placing the scissors under the four threads with the scissor blade to the left of each kloster block. Cut only those threads that run between facing kloster blocks (see the diagram below). Double check before you cut. Remove the threads carefully, leaving a grid of thread.

Cutting the threads

4 Using Coton Perlé no. 8 and tapestry needle size 24, begin needle weaving over the grid of threads (see the diagram). Make a figure-8 under and over the weft threads, placing the needle under and over two threads at a time, and repeat the process until the bar has been filled.

Needle weaving

Worked with traditional kloster blocks, this lovely pattern will inspire stitchers already adept at Hardanger embroidery as well as those new to the method. This is a corner of the placemat.

5 Using no. 8 pearl cotton work the zigzag pattern in double back stitch, working over one block (two threads) of fabric each time. Work from left to right on the diagonal.

6 Still using no. 8 cotton and size 24 tapestry needle, work the border of four-sided stitch from right to left (on the back will be a row of cross stitches).

Straight loops

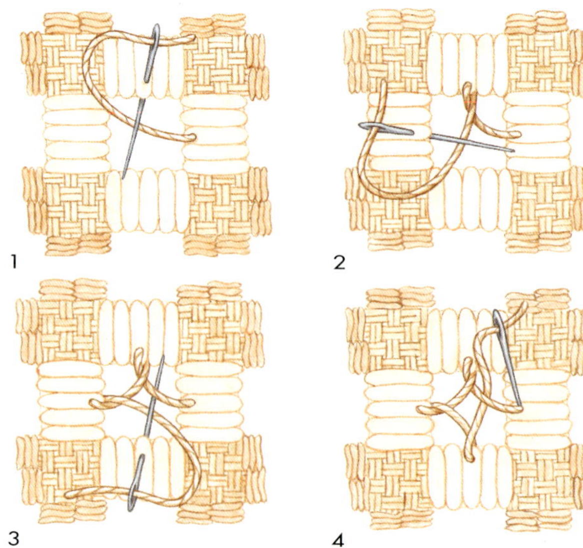

The pattern used for the placemat has been simplified to produce this elegant napkin. Instead of the meander border there is a neat row of buttonhole stitch.

7 Complete the cutwork design by working straight loop stitch in the alternate spaces, as shown on the chart. The diagram at the bottom of page 60 shows how to work this stitch.

8 Using no. 5 cotton and the size 26 needle, work buttonhole stitch around the meander pattern on the edge of the embroidery. Work from left to right, making each buttonhole stitch correspond to each kloster block. At each corner work three stitches into the same hole.

THE NAPKIN

1 Cut a piece of fabric 40 x 40 cm and zigzag or overlock the edges.

2 Following the chart for the napkin on fold-out sheet A, work the embroidery as was described for the placemat.

3 Finish the napkin by working a neat row of buttonhole stitches around all four sides.

TO FINISH

When all the stitching is complete, wash the fabric carefully in lukewarm water and mild detergent and rinse well. While it is still damp, place the cloth stitched side down on a soft towel and press dry.

OPENWORK

Openwork is one of the major classes of embroidery: it includes pulled and drawn thread work as well as the various forms of cutwork. In pulled thread embroidery the stitch being worked pulls the threads together to form an open pattern, while in drawn thread work some threads are drawn out of the fabric and the remaining threads are grouped together. Hem stitch is probably the most commonly used form of drawn thread work. Both these types of embroidery are worked on evenweave fabrics.

Cutwork, on the other hand, requires the use of closely woven fabrics that won't fray easily. Cutwork became fashionable in the sixteenth century and is still very popular. It looks delicate but is in fact sturdy as each part of the design is outlined in close buttonhole stitch. After the buttonhole stitch is worked, parts of the design are cut away and large cut-out areas are bridged with embroidered bars. Some of the forms of cutwork most commonly worked today are:

■ Hardanger cutwork. This is worked on evenweave fabric using a thick cotton or linen thread to build up blocks of geometrical satin stitch (kloster blocks) and squares of cut threads. It originated in the Hardanger district of Norway, hence its name, and was popular in the United States at the turn of the century.

■ Richelieu work. This is another form of cutwork in which picots and buttonhole bars dominate. It is named for a seventeenth century Venetian lace.

■ Broderie anglaise or eyelet embroidery. This became fashionable in the later nineteenth century, developing out of a more delicate white work called Ayrshire embroidery, which incorporated surface stitches and needle lace fillings. It is the holes rather than the areas between that are the main feature of broderie anglaise. Eyelet and teardrop shapes and scalloped edges are traditional and some padded satin stitch is used. A coloured version is known as Madeira work after the island where it developed.

Needlepoint bowl lid

Little needlepoint pictures such as this look completely contemporary, while continuing the traditions of earlier times.

Continental stitch (also called tent stitch) was one of the most popular stitches on eighteenth century needlepoint, and this lovely bowl lid shows why.

Size Embroidery 9 cm diameter
Chart On fold-out sheet E

Stitches

Continental stitch

Materials

- ◆ Bowl
- ◆ 20 x 20 cm of 18-count canvas
- ◆ DMC stranded embroidery cotton in the colours given on the key
- ◆ Appleton's crewel wool in cream (644)
- ◆ Tapestry needle size 22
- ◆ 5 inch embroidery hoop

METHOD

1 Overcast the raw edges of the canvas and fit the hoop over the fabric.
2 Using continental stitch and three strands of cotton, work the design on the graph on fold-out sheet E. For the background use two strands of crewel wool.
3 When it is complete, block it into shape by pressing on the wrong side with a steam iron.
4 Mount the embroidery into the lid following the manufacturer's instructions.

➤ *Roses, daisies and forget-me-nots attract a colourful butterfly on this needlepoint design. It is worked entirely in continental stitch.*

Shadow embroidered coathanger

Antique flowers and waving tendrils make a sweet design motif.

The delicate colours and charming design of the shadow embroidery used here make a very pretty coathanger. It will be perfect for a special garment, whether an heirloom or a favourite you wear often.

Finished size Length 42 cm
Pattern and motif On fold-out sheet F

Stitches

Double back stitch
Ladder stitch
Stem stitch

Materials

- 40 cm wooden hanger
- 50 cm of ivory cotton voile
- 20 cm of 5 mm clear plastic piping
- 20 cm Pellon
- 50 cm medium wadding
- 1 m of 3 mm wide ivory ribbon
- 1.5 m ivory satin piping
- Mill Hill Glass Seed Beads in blue (2006)
- Quilting needle size 10
- HB pencil
- Plastic embroidery hoop
- DMC stranded embroidery cotton in antique mauve (316), light antique mauve (778), old gold (677), antique blue (931), light antique blue (932), green-grey (3053)
- Machine thread to match voile
- Tracing paper

EMBROIDERY

1 Trace the coathanger pattern on fold-out sheet F onto tracing paper. Use the soft pencil to transfer it to the fabric, placing the front on the bias and the back on the straight grain. A seam allowance of 6 mm has been included. Do not cut out the pieces.

2 Trace the embroidery design onto tracing paper and tape it to a window or light box. Tape the fabric over it so the design is on the front of the hanger. Use a pencil to transfer the design to the fabric.

3 Place the fabric in the embroidery hoop and work as described.

■ The shadow work is embroidered from the right side of the fabric using double back stitch and one strand of embroidery cotton in the quilting needle. Always start with a waste knot. Bring the needle to the front approximately 2 mm from the tip of a petal and then put it in at the tip. Continue stitching from side to side, using small back stitches. On the curve, adjust the stitches so that they are smaller on the inside curve and larger on the outside.

■ Where the petals share a common line you will need to pick up the threads at the back of the work. On the unworked side make your stitch through the fabric as usual, then turn to the back of the work and put the needle around a finished stitch in order to bring the thread back to the other side. Finish off each thread on the wrong side, as close as possible to the edge.

■ Embroider the petals of the central flower in alphabetical order, and remember to finish one before you move on to the next. For petals A and B use green-grey (3035), for C, D, E and F use old gold (677), for G and H use antique blue (931), for I use light antique mauve (778) and for J and K use antique mauve (316).

■ Embroider the side flowers in the same way but work J and K before I.

4 The stem and leaves at the base of each design are embroidered using green-grey (3053).

The shadow work on this lovely coathanger is embroidered from the right side of the fabric using stranded embroidery cottons in muted antique shades. Tiny glass beads add texture without interfering with the function of the hanger.

5 Work the tendrils in stem stitch using one strand of light antique blue (932). Sew a glass bead to the ends of the tendrils.

MAKING THE HANGER

1 Check that no loose threads show outside the design. Lay the embroidery face down on a thick towel and iron it carefully. Cut out the front.

2 Cut two pieces of Pellon the same size as the pattern on the straight grain. Pin one piece of Pellon to the wrong side of the front. With the raw edges even, pin the piping to the right side, starting where the hook will go with a bit of overlap at the end of the piping. Curve the piping evenly around the edge of the fabric, making small snips in the bias around the curves. Stitch along the stitching on the piping and across the overlapped section.

3 Cut out the back. Pin the second piece of Pellon to the wrong side of the back and stitch the lower edge. With right sides together and raw edges matching, pin the front to the back and tack it together. Starting at the centre top (but leaving space for the hook) stitch along the top and around the end. Repeat on the other side. Do not stitch across the bottom.

4 Cut a 20 cm piece of satin piping to cover the hook of the hanger. Unpick it, discard the cord, press the fabric flat, fold it in half and sew a 6 mm seam down the length of the fabric to make a tube 1.2 cm wide. If the piping did not have a generous seam allowance you may have to join two pieces to make an equivalent tube. Trim excess off the top. Turn right side out. Cut the plastic piping to fit the hook, slip the satin tube over the piping so that it fits snugly. Trim the fabric to 5 mm at the base of the plastic tube and push the fabric ends into it. Push the plastic tube over the hook until it sits flat on the wood.

5 Cut the wadding to an 8 cm strip and starting at the hook, wrap it firmly around the wooden hanger. Place an extra piece of wadding at the ends. Repeat this two or three times, using a slip stitch where necessary to hold it in place. Repeat on the other end of the hanger. The result should be firm and even, with no lumps.

6 Place the padded hanger in the cover. You may need to stuff extra wadding into the ends. Pin the edges together and ladder stitch the opening closed. Cut two 50 cm lengths of 3 mm wide ribbon and tie a bow around the hook.

Honeycomb smocked nightdress

Seed pearls accentuate the honeycomb pattern of the smocking.

Smocking, or ornamental stitching over gathers, may have traditionally been used on the smocks of farm workers but this beautiful nightdress shows just how elegant a contemporary version of the technique can be.

Size To fit bust 89–94 cm (size 10–12)

Stitches

Honeycomb smocking

Materials

- ◆ 3 m of 120 cm wide white handkerchief linen
- ◆ Four sheets Semco yellow 6 mm smocking dots
- ◆ Machine thread in white and a contrasting colour
- ◆ DMC Flower Thread in white (5 skeins)
- ◆ Crewel needles sizes 7/9
- ◆ Approximately 40 cm of 12 mm wide elastic
- ◆ Maria George white seed pearls (6 packets)

CUTTING OUT

Pull a thread across one end of the linen to find the straight grain and cut one length 127 x 120 cm for the front and one length 127 x 80 cm for the back. Also from linen cut two strips 110 x 10 cm on the straight grain for the waist ties, one bias strip 50 cm long and 3 cm wide on the fold for the upper edge of the front, and four strips 50 x 4 cm for the shoulder straps. See the cutting diagram on page 68.

Front and back views

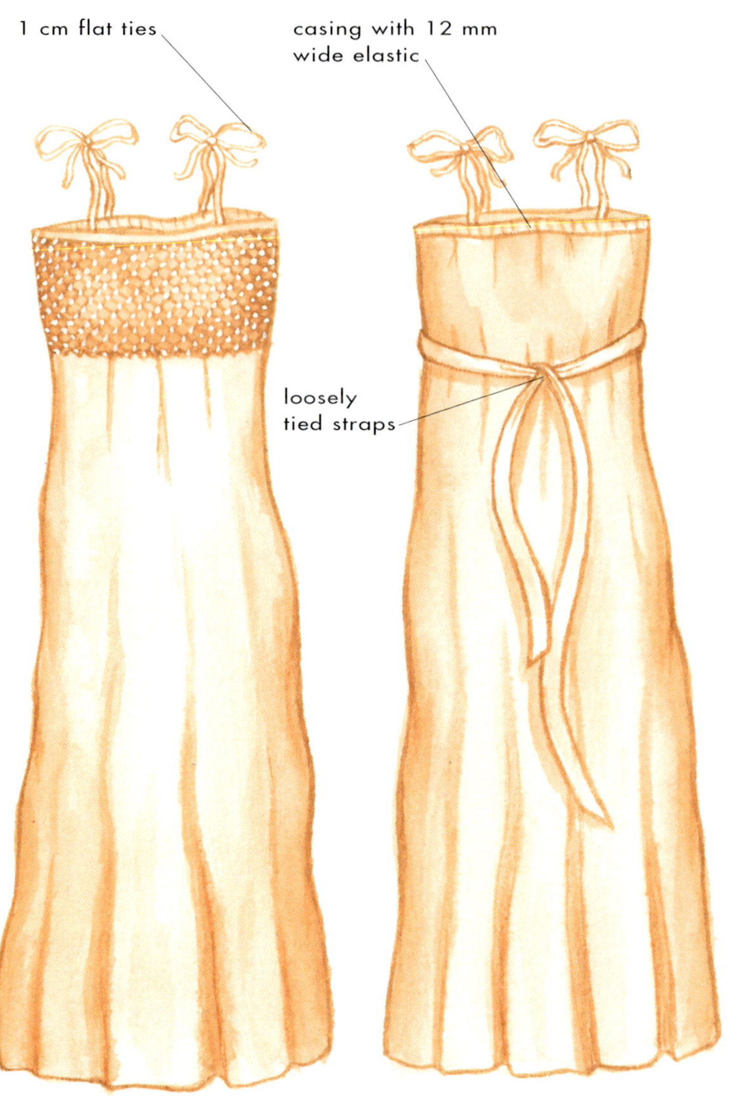

SMOCKING THE FRONT

1 Take the large piece of linen and press any creases from it. Decide on the required depth of the honeycombing (we made ours 24 cm). Place it wrong side up and lay the smocking dots on it, wax side down. Leave 1.5 cm on each side for the side seams and 2 cm at the top. Butt the strips of dots together, taking care to match the dots exactly. When you are sure the dots are all matched, press them onto the

➤ *The smocked bodice of this beautiful nightdress reaches to slightly above the waist, and a comfortable fit is ensured by the elastic threaded through the back and by the ties at the back.*

Cutting diagram

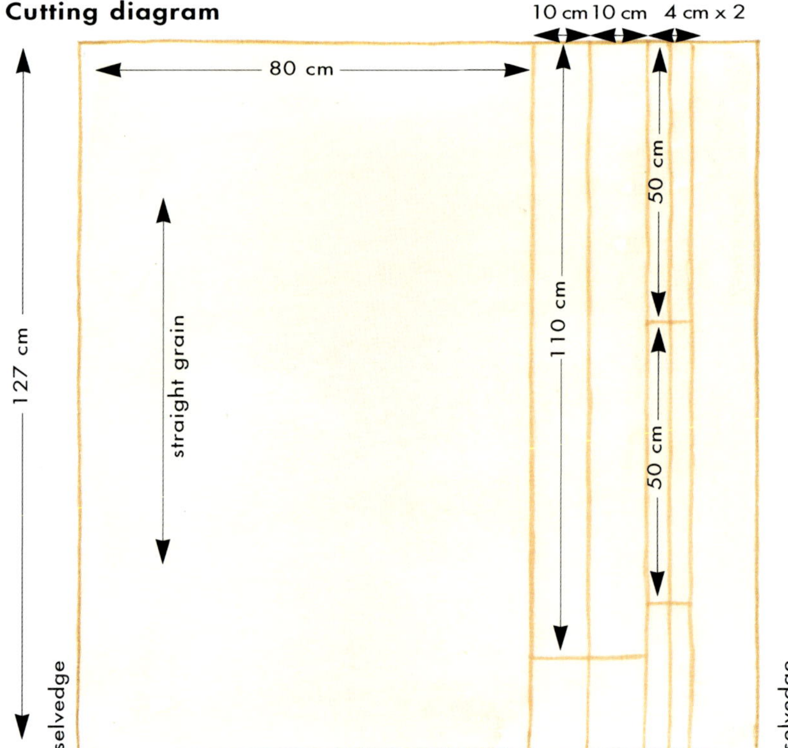

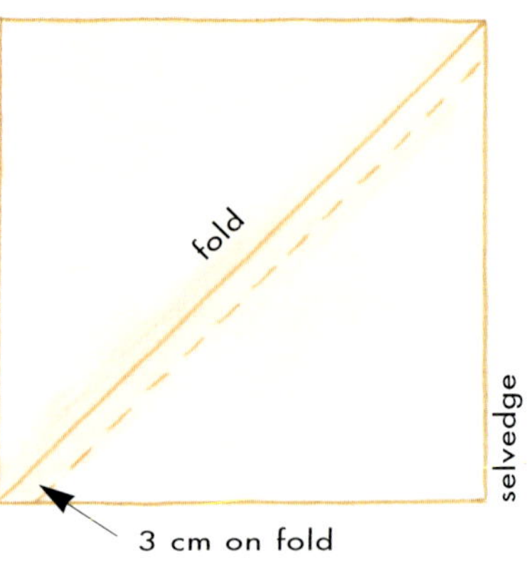

material—be careful not to move the iron from side to side as the dots will move and blur (see the manufacturer's instructions).

2 Using the machine thread (it should be a colour that stands out clearly against the fabric), pick up the dots, taking a few threads at the same time. Continue until all the dots are picked up. Tie the threads together in pairs along the left-hand side and then gather the fabric in until it fits across the bust, reaching from side seam to side seam. Pull the gathers a little tighter and tie the threads in pairs at the right-hand side. Adjust the gathers until they are evenly spaced across the fabric.

3 With the flower thread, work double rows of honeycomb smocking across the right side of the fabric, using the coloured machine thread as a guide and adjusting the gathers as you go (see the stitching diagram for honeycomb smocking at right). Starting at the left-hand edge of the fabric, join the first two gathers with two back stitches, then bring the needle from the back to the row below and join the second and third gathers in the same way. Return to the first row and join the third and fourth gathers with two back stitches and so on to the end of the rows. Repeat this process for as many double rows as is necessary to cover the area.

The bodice is smocked in a honeycomb pattern and then the seed pearls are stitched on in a diamond pattern.

A small loop of thread is left between each pearl attachment.

Honeycomb smocking

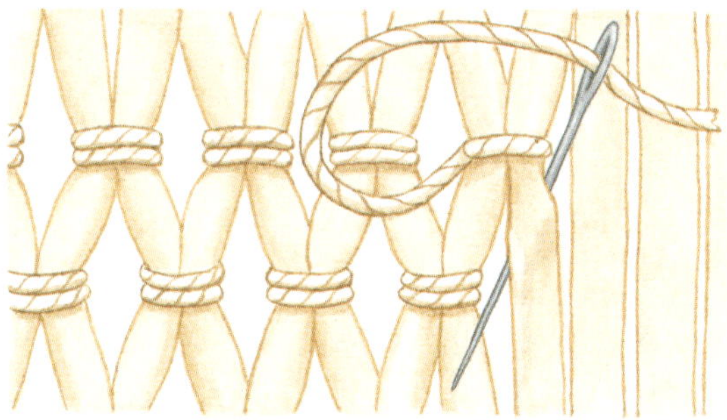

ASSEMBLING THE NIGHTDRESS

1 When the honeycombing is complete, remove all the coloured threads except for the top row. Measure across your body from underarm to underarm, and adjust the remaining coloured thread to match the measurement, loosening it as appropriate.

2 Take the folded bias strip, open it out and, with right sides together, pin one long edge across the top of the front just above the top row of honeycombing. Check that the length of the top fits the underarm measurement and machine stitch in position. A 1 cm seam allowance has been allowed on the strip. Fold the strip over the raw edge, turn in the long edge and, with tiny stitches slip stitch it to the machine stitches.

3 Waist ties. Take one 10 cm wide strip and, with right sides together, fold it in half lengthwise to form a tie. Stitch across one end and along the side, using 1 cm seams. Trim corners and pull through to the right side. Repeat on the other tie. Press the ties carefully and lay them aside.

4 Shoulder straps. Fold each of the four 4 cm wide strips lengthwise with right sides together. Machine across one end and down the side. Trim corners and pull ties through. Press carefully and lay aside.

5 Back. Make a 1.75 cm wide casing across the top of the back and stitch along close to the top edge. Thread a piece of elastic through the casing. Adjust it to fit from side seam to side seam and stitch the sides of the casing closed, stitching through the elastic.

6 Place the front and back together with right sides facing and pin the side seams, inserting the waist ties level with the bottom of the honeycombing. Stitch the side seams and finish with overlocker or zigzag stitch. Make a 1.5 cm wide hem around the bottom.

7 Place the shoulder straps where comfortable at the top back and front and stitch them in position by hand, being careful not to stitch into the elastic.

ADDING THE PEARLS

Using flower thread and a fine needle, stitch the pearls to the honeycombing in a diamond pattern. In order not to restrict the elasticity of the bodice, take a tiny stitch on each side of each pearl on the back and leave a small (1 cm) loop of thread between each pearl.

SMOCKING

Smocking is a type of decorative stitching used to gather fabric. The technique can be traced back to at least the sixth century but the term comes from the old English *smocc*. A smock was a loose outer garment worn by agricultural workers to protect their clothes. They were especially popular in the late seventeenth and eighteenth centuries. Smocked garments were also worn by women, at first as underclothes but then as outer garments too. Smocking was particularly fashionable during the early twentieth century.

Smocking is based on a grid of dots that are marked on the fabric. In traditional smocking the dots were marked on the wrong side of the fabric, running stitches were worked from dot to dot to gather the fabric into pleats and then smocking stitches were worked on the right side. 'Mock' smocking is now more common: the dots are marked on the right side and smocking is worked from dot to dot.

Cross-stitch garden picture

The tiny glass beads stitched into the design catch the light in the same way droplets of water from a fountain would.

Cross stitch on linen has always been a popular combination for embroidered pictures and this delightful parterre garden is no exception. The scene is highlighted with eyelet stitches to indicate the shrubs, and tiny purple beads are grouped in the centre as if gushing up from a fountain.

Finished size Embroidery approximately 19 x 17 cm
Chart On fold-out sheet C

Stitches

Back stitch
Cross stitch
Eyelet stitch

Material

- 40 x 40 cm of ecru Belfast linen with 12 threads to 1 cm (or ecru Dublin linen with 10 threads to 1 cm)
- Ginnie Thompson Flower Thread in the colours given on the colour key, plus fawn (700, or DMC 3782) and olive green (409, or DMC 3011)
- Tapestry needle size 24
- Maria George beads in three shades of purple: DBR 23, 59 and 135 (Mill Hill beads 3037, 252 and 3034 can be substituted but are slightly larger)
- Beading needle
- Beading or quilting cotton, either clear or to match the beads or background

STITCHING ON LINEN

■ Stitching on linen is no more difficult than stitching on Aida cloth but the method used is different. Do not look for holes into which to stitch. Count two threads up and two across and put in the needle. Then lift two threads on the needle and pull the needle through. Repeat for a row of cross-stitch understitches.

■ Do not use a hoop or frame. It is unnecessary and if you use one you will tend to sew with a stabbing motion rather than a sewing one. Using a regular sewing motion will regulate your tension, too. You can check your tension by seeing that there are no obvious holes in the linen—if there are, you are pulling too tightly.

■ Prevent the thread twisting and knotting by turning your needle a quarter turn each time you bring it through the fabric. Turn anti-clockwise if you are right-handed and clockwise if you are left-handed. This twist counteracts the twisting movement.

➤ *This parterre garden picture is worked in cross stitch on linen using flower threads that match the weight and thickness of the linen. The even texture is a perfect background for the intense colours of the threads.*

FLOWER THREADS

Each type of flower thread has a different colour range and so the result shown in our picture cannot be guaranteed unless you use the Ginnie Thompson Flower Threads recommended. However, if you are not able to obtain them, the picture can be worked in Danish Flower Thread (or even DMC stranded cotton).

Linens with ten or twelve threads to the centimetre are worked with one strand of Ginnie Thompson Flower Thread or Danish Flower Thread. DMC stranded cotton is thinner and you will need two or three strands to cover the fabric adequately. If you are using one of these alternate threads, work a small square on a corner of the fabric to determine how many strands you will need to use.

– plant a garden – plant a garden –
if you would be happy for the rest of your life –
if you would be happy for the rest of your life –

Texts and proverbs were often worked into nineteenth century embroideries. This verse continues the tradition, in modern style.

WORKING THE EMBROIDERY

1 Before you begin to embroider, overlock the edges of the fabric to prevent fraying. Find the centre of the fabric: this will be the centre of the garden. Count up twelve stitches and one stitch to the left. Begin stitching the outline of the garden here. The chart is on fold-out sheet C.

2 Using one strand of Ginnie Thompson Flower Thread, begin stitching the outlines of the gardens. Follow the graph and work as far as possible from left to right and downwards as this way you avoid rubbing your hand over the completed work.

3 After the garden edges, stitch the fence. The tops of the gateposts are curved and are stitched in donkey brown (720), using either back stitch with a quarter stitch inside or six three-quarter stitches for each post. This is easy on linen as you separate the threads.

4 Complete the cross stitching as shown.

5 Eyelet stitches form points of emphasis throughout the garden. Each is worked in an anti-clockwise way, with each stitch worked from the outside into the centre. Pull gently on each stitch to eventually form the eyelet hole. Stitch the number of spokes indicated on the chart, and stitch over two threads or four as appropriate. The eight large eyelets outside the back stitch diamond are worked in dark olive green (470); and the eight small eyelets in the top corner gardens are all dark green (451). The eight large eyelets inside the diamond are light green (439), while in the central garden the diamond pattern of small eyelets are dark green (451) and the four small corner eyelets are light green (439).

6 Once the eyelets are completed, work the remaining back stitch, working each stitch over two threads. The diamond is worked in fawn (700), the gate in dark olive green (470) and the writing in olive green (409). The initials of the stitcher and the year can be added at the bottom.

7 The glass beads are now attached to the picture. Follow the graph for their placement. To attach each bead, make the under stitch by stitching through the fabric, thread on the bead and then stitch the over stitch. You can anchor it with a holding stitch at the back if desired.

TO FINISH

1 Gently wash the embroidery with a pure soap (not detergent or wool wash) and rinse several times. Gently squeeze to remove excess water. Hold the wet work against a white surface and check to see if there is a halo of bled colour around the stitching—if so, soak it in a bucket of cold water for several hours and then repeat the check. Roll it in a white towel and pat dry. While the embroidery is still damp, place it face down under a cloth and iron it dry.

2 Frame the picture as desired.

NEEDLEPOINT

Needlepoint is a type of embroidery in which the stitches are worked over the threads of a linen or cotton evenweave canvas. The canvas can have a single or double mesh. This sort of embroidery is often called 'tapestry' because it originally imitated woven tapestries.

Until the early nineteenth century, needlepoint was known as canvas work. It was made at least as early as the Middle Ages, when it was known as *opus pulvinarium*, or cushion work. It was, however, in the seventeenth century that it became popular, for with its canvas base it formed a strong fabric suitable for the upholstered furniture and hangings then in vogue.

Needlepoint worked on a fine canvas with sixteen or more holes to a linear inch is called petit point. If the canvas has between seven and sixteen holes to the inch it is called gros point, and if it has less than seven holes, quick point. Until the eighteenth century most needlepoint was petit point and it was worked on very fine canvas with up to forty-five squares per inch.

There are over 150 stitches used for needlepoint. The ones most often used are tent stitch (also called continental stitch), which covers one square diagonally, and cross stitch, which in its simplest form is worked from left to right and back again, with the first 'run' creating a row of diagonal or half cross stitches and the second 'run' completing the crosses. Cross stitch is the stitch traditionally used on gros point.

Assisi embroidery is a very old form of embroidery associated with the Italian town of that name and traditionally worked in bright red or blue on cream linen. In this form of embroidery the design areas are left unworked and the background is filled with cross stitches. The design is often emphasised by stitching around it with Holbein stitch.

Also popular is needlepoint using Florentine stitch (also called flame, bargello or Hungarian stitch), which is worked vertically in wavy, zigzag patterns in shaded colours. These patterns originated in Hungary during the Middle Ages and were used in decorations for the Bargello Palace in Florence.

Berlin woolwork is another specific form of needlepoint that was extremely popular in Europe and America during the nineteenth century. Patterns were printed on squared paper and coloured so that they were easy to follow and transfer to canvas. This wool embroidery was worked in tent or cross stitch.

Lingerie bag with trapunto violets

Trapunto shadow work, a form of quilting, is used to form the bunch of violets on this lingerie bag. The simple design is perfect to show off the combination of relief and shadow embroidery, and yet the technique is remarkably simple to execute.

Finished size 44 x 30 cm (without lace)
Embroidery motif On fold-out sheet B

Stitches

Running stitch

Materials

- 70 cm of ivory cotton batiste
- DMC stranded embroidery cotton in light shell pink (224), very light avocado green (471), light blue violet (340), dark blue-violet (330), cream (712)
- DMC tapestry wool in dark pink (7195), light pink (7192), dark green (7344), medium green (7342), light green (7341), violet (7242)
- Quilting needle size 10
- Tapestry needle size 20
- Mill Hill Glass Seed Beads in yellow (00128)
- 2 m of 3 mm wide double-sided satin ribbon in green
- 2 m of 3 mm wide double-sided satin ribbon in violet
- 3.5 m of 3 mm wide double-sided satin ribbon in pink
- 95 cm of 25 mm ivory cotton edging lace
- Machine thread
- Tracing paper
- Black pen
- Sharp lead pencil

PREPARATION

1 Cut two pieces of batiste 92 x 33 cm. Put them together and stitch the long sides with French seams.

➤ *The delicate colours of the violets and bow on this beautiful lingerie bag are achieved by threading strongly coloured wools behind the sheer cotton batiste.*

2 Fold the double piece in half with the seams matching to form the bag. With a pin, mark the centre of the cut (bottom) edge. Measure up 14 cm from that point and mark with a pin to indicate where the centre of the bow will be ('x' on the motif on fold-out sheet B). Either side of the first pin, measure up 11 cm from the edge and mark with pins to indicate where the lower loops of the bow will be.
3 Trace the design on the fold-out sheet onto the tracing paper using the black pen. Place the tracing paper between the two layers of batiste, lining it up on the pins, and trace lightly over the design using the lead pencil. Remove the paper and pins.
4 Tack the two layers of batiste together in a grid pattern so that they do not move.

EMBROIDERY

1 All the embroidery is worked with a single strand of embroidery cotton and the quilter's needle. Start with a waste knot and slide the needle between the layers of batiste, coming up on the pencil line. Give the thread a light tug so that the knot is between both layers. Quilt the design with small running stitches and finish off by winding the thread twice around the needle, insering the needle between the two layers of batiste, tightening the wraps and pulling through. Tug the thread so that the knot is between the layers. Outline the bow with light shell pink (224), the leaves with very light avocado green (471) and the violets with light blue-violet (340). When the stitching is complete, remove the tacking stitches.
2 Turn the bag to the wrong side and thread the tapestry needle with the appropriate tapestry wool (see the key). Fill each outlined shape with wool by piercing the batiste with the needle and passing it between the two layers. Cut off the wool as close as possible to the batiste. Use the tip of the needle to hide the ends inside the padded area and gently stroke the batiste threads to close the holes. Do not overstuff the design. Hold the finished piece up to the light to check if you need to add more wool.

Threading the wool

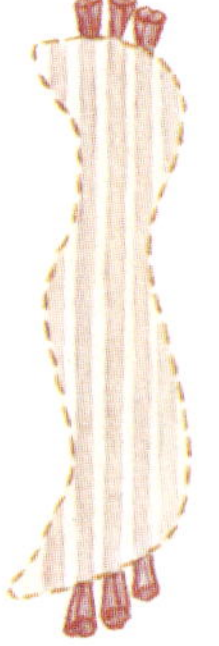

TRAPUNTO SHADOW WORK

Trapunto shadow work is an embroidery technique derived from quilting. In quilting several layers of fabric are sewn together to form pocketed insulation and padding. The stitching can form simple lattice or lozenge patterns, or can be more elaborate.

Quilting probably developed in China. It then spread to western Asia where the Crusaders saw and adopted it as part of their armour. In the sixteenth and seventeenth centuries it was widely used for garments as well as bed hangings and coverings, and the decorative designs included complex geometric patterns and foliage. In the eighteenth century it formed the background for rich embroidery in silks and metallic threads. 'False' quilting, which is not padded, has been popular since the seventeenth century.

Trapunto, or stuffed, quilting uses padded areas to make relief patterns. The design is stitched through two pieces of fabric, a slit is made in the under piece and stuffing is inserted before the slit is stitched closed. Italian quilting is similar, except that the design consists of parallel lines of stitching with the padding inserted between them. Both types of quilting are adapted to shadow work by using strongly coloured wadding or wool, and sheer fabrics.

MAKING THE BAG

1 Close the bottom of the bag with a French seam.
2 Join the cut ends of the lace with a seam to form a circle. Pull a thread in the lace heading and gather to fit the top of the bag. Pin the lace on and whip onto the top edge of the bag.

TO FINISH

1 Using cream (712) stranded embroidery cotton work a few straight stitches on each of the violet petals. Then work three straight stitches in dark

The outlines of the design are stitched through two layers of fabric with stranded embroidery cottons and then the design areas are filled with tapestry wool to create this beautiful trapunto shadow work design.

blue-violet (330) on the lower petal. Sew a yellow bead in the centre of each violet.

2 From the pink ribbon cut two 1 m lengths and twelve 12 cm lengths. Place the 1 m lengths aside. Knot both ends of the 12 cm pieces. Fold each in half and pin them to the bag with the folded top of the ribbon 5 cm down from the top of the bag and 5 cm apart. Stitch across them 1 cm down from the folded top and 1.5 cm further down to form the casing.

3 Cut the lengths of green and violet ribbon in half. Thread three 1 m ribbons (one pink, one green and one violet) through the casing and tie them together with an overhand knot. Also tie a knot in each end of each of the individual ribbons. Thread the other three ribbons (pink, green and violet) through the casing in the opposite direction, tie them together with an overhand knot and then tie knots in the ends of each individual ribbon.

Wreath of roses shoe stuffers

Bullion stitch roses form the basis of this dainty design, which is enclosed by tendrils stem stitched in gold thread.

Dusky pink satin and a design that harks back to eighteenth century elegance make these shoe stuffers just perfect. Putting on your shoes will become a real event when it means you have first to remove these lovely items.

Finished size Length approximately 17 cm
Pattern and embroidery motif On fold-out sheet B

Stitches

Bullion stitch
French knot
Whipped back stitch

Materials

- ◆ 30 cm of dusky pink satin
- ◆ Madeira stranded silk in dark pink (0812), medium pink (0813) and light pink (0815)
- ◆ Caron Waterlilies stranded silk in olive
- ◆ Caron Impressions silk/wool in blue (7005) and yellow (4005)
- ◆ Madeira Metallic Thread no. 12 in gold (33)
- ◆ Straw needles sizes 7/9
- ◆ Crewel needles sizes 3/9
- ◆ 55 cm of 15 mm wide edging lace
- ◆ 40 cm of 7 mm wide double-sided satin ribbon
- ◆ 20 cm embroidery hoop
- ◆ Polyester fibre fill
- ◆ Dried lavender
- ◆ Tracing paper
- ◆ Black pen
- ◆ Sharp lead pencil
- ◆ Machine thread to match fabric

PREPARATION

1 Trace the pattern and design on fold-out sheet B onto tracing paper using the black pen. Mark the centres of the roses, the forget-me-nots and the leaves. Trace the design again, mirror-imaged, so that you have a pair.

➤ *A little dried lavender added to the filling makes these shoe stuffers fragrant as well as beautiful. They'll keep your shoes smelling sweet as well as in good shape.*

Bullion roses

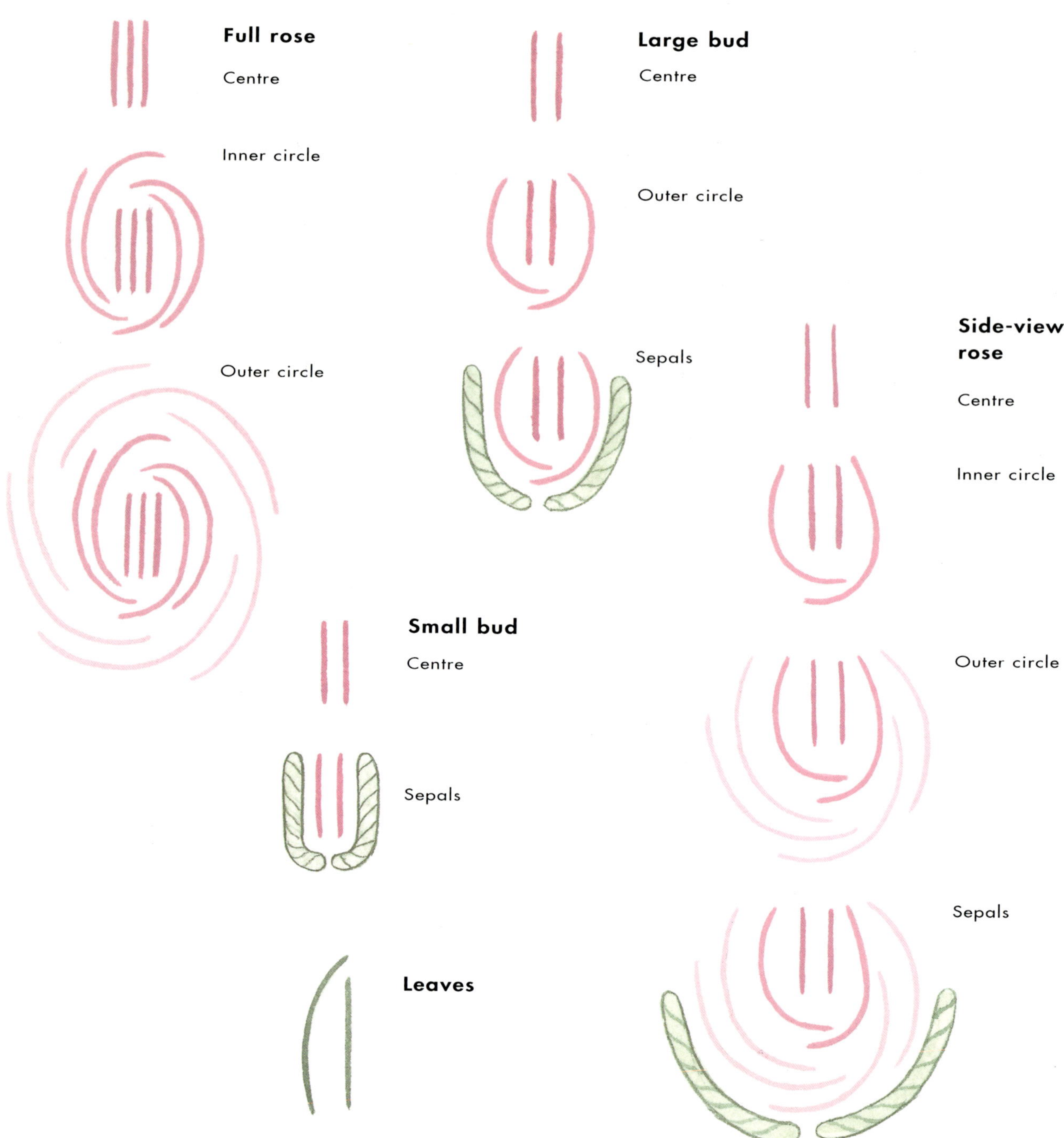

2 Tape the tracings to a window or light box, tape the fabric over them with right side facing you. Trace the design and cutting line lightly with the lead pencil. Untape the fabric but do not cut out until the embroidery is finished. Place in hoop.

EMBROIDERY

All the embroidery is worked with one strand of thread. Embroider the bullion stitch roses using the size 7 straw needle. For the leaves and sepals use the size 9 straw needle. See the diagrams above.

■ *One full rose.* Work the centre with dark pink silk using three bullion stitches of twelve twists. For the inner circle use medium pink and four bullion stitches of 14–16 twists. For the outer circle use light pink and five bullion stitches of 14–16 twists.

■ *Three side-view roses.* For the centre use dark pink silk and two bullion stitches of twelve twists. For the

A touch of gold thread and dainty silks provide just the right decoration for these exquisite satin shoe stuffers.

inner circle use medium pink and two bullion stitches of fourteen twists and for the outer circle light pink and four bullion stitches of fourteen twists. Work the sepals in olive Waterlilies silk with two bullion stitches of twelve twists.

■ *Three large buds.* For the centre use dark pink and two bullion stitches of twelve twists, for the outer circle use medium pink silk and two bullion stitches of fourteen twists. For the sepals use olive and two bullion stitches of ten twists.

■ *Two small buds.* Work the centre in dark pink silk using two bullion stitches with eight twists. Work the sepals in olive Waterlilies silk using two bullion stitches of eight twists.

■ *Leaves.* Using olive silk, work the leaves with one straight bullion stitch of eight twists and then curve another bullion stitch of ten twists around the straight bullion stitch.

■ *Forget-me-nots.* For the centre work one French knot, one twist, using yellow silk/wool and a crewel needle. For the petals, use five French knots, one twist, in blue silk/wool.

■ *Goldwork.* Use one strand of metallic gold thread, a crewel needle and small back stitches. Whip around them with one thread of gold.

MAKING UP

1 Cut out the two fronts along the cutting lines. Also cut out two shapes from the satin fabric to form the backs of the stuffers.

2 With the right sides of a front and a back piece together, machine stitch each pair with a 6 mm seam. Turn the shoe stuffers to the right side. Turn the tops over on the fold line. Press. Run a gathering thread around on the gathering line.

3 Cut the lace in half and join the cut ends to form two circles. Whip one circle of lace onto the fold line of each stuffer.

4 Fill the toe firmly with the polyester fibre fill. Wrap the lavender in some of the fibre fill and place in the middle. Fill firmly up to the gathering line. Pull the gathering thread up firmly to close the shoe stuffer.

5 Cut the ribbon in half and tie a bow around each gathered top.

Candlewick wedding set

The keepsake box is lined with homespun, which is held in place by colonial knots. A ribbon hinge supports the lid.

The glossy white thread of the candlewick embroidery forms a subtle contrast on the white homespun cotton used for this unusual wedding set. The little ring cushion is just the right size for the flower girl or pageboy, while the box will keep your wedding mementoes safe for years to come.

Finished size Keepsake box 35 x 24 cm and embroidered panel 30 x 19 cm; ring cushion 18 x 13 cm
Embroidery designs On fold-out sheet F

Stitches

Chain stitch
Colonial knot
Detached chain stitch
Feather stitch
Stem stitch

Materials

- White homespun cotton
- Tracing paper
- Black pen
- Pencil or water-soluble pen
- Coton Perlé no. 5 in white (2 skeins)
- DMC stranded embroidery cotton in white
- Crewel needle size 7

Cushion

- 80 cm of white satin piping
- 60 cm of 5 mm wide white ribbon
- Filling

Box

- Craftwood box 35 x 24 x 8 cm
- Folk Art Sealer

➤ *White-on-white is a perfect scheme for these charming wedding items. Contrast comes from the glossy pearl cotton and satin piping seen against the matt homespun fabric.*

in the Great Hall at Mount Broughton
Kater Road, Sutton Forest
36 Valerie Avenue

Simple designs are the essence of candlewicking and what could be more simple, or more effective, than this.

- FolkArt basecoat in Wicker White
- FolkArt Pearl Cote, Pearl Glaze
- Spray adhesive
- Craft glue
- Cardboard 1 mm thick
- Masking tape
- 1.2 m white satin piping
- 1 m of 1.5 cm wide white ribbon
- 40 cm medium wadding

RING CUSHION

1 Cut two pieces of homespun 23 x 18 cm. Trace the ring cushion design and the relevant initials from fold-out sheet F onto tracing paper with a black pen. Tape it to a window or light box and tape one piece of fabric over it. Transfer the design to the fabric using a water-soluble pen.

2 Work all the design apart from the date in Coton Perlé. The initials are embroidered in stem stitch for the thin lines and chain stitch for the thicker sections. The hearts and other dots are colonial knots, and the stems are worked in feather stitch. Finally, add the date, using two strands of stranded cotton and small stem stitch.

3 When the embroidery is completed, wash it gently to remove the pen or pencil marks, place it face down on a soft towel and iron it.

4 Leaving a seam allowance of about 2 cm, tack piping around the edge of the right side of the embroidered piece, beginning and ending at the centre of the bottom. Place the front and back together with right sides facing and stitch them, leaving an opening for turning. Turn right side out and fill. Stitch the opening closed.

5 Cut three 20 cm lengths of ribbon. Tie one in a bow and stitch it over the join in the piping. Stitch the centre of the other pieces one on either side of the initials, ready for the rings.

KEEPSAKE BOX

1 Cut one piece of homespun 32 x 22 cm. Transfer the design and relevant initials from fold-out sheet F. Work the embroidery as for the ring cushion, using detached chain stitch for the flowers.

2 Seal the box, and paint it inside and out with three or four coats of white paint. Let it dry thoroughly and apply three or four light sprays of pearl glaze.

3 To line the box, cut out pieces of cardboard to fit the bottom and each side of the box and the lid (ten pieces) and pieces of wadding to match. On the base pieces for box and lid mark a grid in pencil and use an upholstery needle or nail to pierce through at each intersection (this makes it easier to add the colonial knots later). Glue the cardboard to the wadding.

Hearts make the perfect decoration for a wedding set. The initials of bride and groom, and the date of the wedding, complete the concept.

4 Cut a piece of homespun to match each cardboard piece but allow 2 cm extra all around each piece of fabric. Press the fabric pieces. Add craft glue around the edges of one cardboard piece, place it wadding side down on the corresponding fabric and fold the edges of the fabric over the cardboard, long sides first. Keeping the fabric taut, fold in the corners and then the sides. Repeat on all pieces.
5 Tape the end of a long piece of Coton Perlé to the back of the cardboard lining for the lid base. At the first hole, bring the needle through the cardboard and fabric, and make a colonial knot. Return the needle to the back of the cardboard and tape the thread to the cardboard. Repeat this at each hole in the lid base and then at each hole in the box base.
6 Take the embroidered piece for the top of the box and prepare it as for the lining pieces. Add glue around the edge of the cardboard and press piping onto it, starting at the centre front. Overlap the piping at the join.
7 Cut two pieces of ribbon 35 cm long and glue and tape them to the inside of the box and lid, in the centre of the front long sides. Cut a 30 cm long piece of ribbon and fix it across one corner so that the lid does not fall back when opened.
8 Place glue on the back of the base lining piece and fit it into the box. Repeat the process for the long sides and then for the short ones. Repeat for the lid. Centre the embroidered piece on top of the lid and glue it in place.

CANDLEWICK EMBROIDERY

Candlewick embroidery was first made by the early European settlers in America in the early eighteenth century and later by the colonists in Australia. They brought their embroidery skills with them from Europe but in the new lands materials were limited and most settlers were poor. They had to use whatever was available. As fabric they used empty flour bags that had been bleached in the sun, and for embroidery thread they used the cotton from candle wicks. Only a few stitches were used, and the designs were kept very simple.

Today, candlewicking is regaining popularity but it is now worked in a range of materials and threads. Usually the work is white on white or cream on cream, but coloured materials and threads are sometimes used. The range of threads used has also widened and includes candlewick cotton, stranded cotton and pearl thread. Stem, satin and chain stitches are the main stitches, along with the characteristic colonial knot. Many of the traditional patterns are still used, and hearts feature prominently in the repertoire.

Caring for your embroidery

Like all textiles, embroidered pieces will gradually deteriorate, but the process will be faster or slower according to the treatment they receive. By taking care when using, cleaning and storing your pieces, you will prolong their life until they truly become family heirlooms.

WORKING THE EMBROIDERY

■ Begin by always choosing good quality fabrics and threads. They will last longer, as well as giving a better result.

■ Keep your work as clean as possible. Body oils and dirt from your fingers can stain the fabric, and so always wash your hands before working on the embroidery or even handling it. Keep the embroidery folded away in a bag or work basket when you are not stitching.

■ Remove the hoop each time you stop stitching to prevent it marking the work.

Diagonal stitches such as continental stitch will distort the canvas, which will need to be blocked—or damp stretched—to return it to its proper squared shape.

■ Never leave the needle inserted in the fabric. If you don't get back to your embroidery for some time, the needle could leave rust marks.

■ Don't leave your embroidery in strong sunlight or under very bright lights as the light can fade colours and weaken the threads. Heat, too, will damage textiles: around 17°C is a good temperature for keeping fabric in good condition.

■ Damp will also damage fabrics and threads, so keep embroidered pieces in a dark, dry place when they are not being worked on.

WASHING EMBROIDERY

Washing embroidery can cause irreparable damage, but it is sometimes necessary. Always wash embroidered pieces by hand and it is best to wash each piece separately.

■ Test a small piece of embroidery first to check that it is colourfast.

■ Wash in lukewarm water with a mild soap. Do not use strong detergents.

■ Rinse in clear water. If the colour runs, keep rinsing until the water is clear.

■ Roll the embroidery between two clean towels, squeeze gently but do not wring. Unroll the towels and spread the embroidery out flat to dry on a towel.

■ If the fabric is not washable, use a stain remover to remove marks but test it first on a scrap of the fabric.

■ Embroidery should not usually be dry-cleaned. If dry-cleaning is essential, explain to the dry-cleaner that there may be a reaction between the thread dyes and the dry-cleaning chemicals.

PRESSING EMBROIDERY

To iron an embroidered piece, place it face down on a clean towel and place a clean cloth over it. If the piece is dry, use a damp cloth. Press with a warm steam iron, and avoid ironing preparations or protectors as they may cause a chemical reaction with thread dyes.

BLOCKING

If the embroidery has been distorted by the stitching, it will need to be blocked, that is, stretched while damp to restore its shape. First, select a board large enough to take the whole piece and cover it with

After the christening this beautiful gown will need to be stored until it is needed for the next baby. Wash and iron it carefully, then roll it in tissue paper before placing it in a cardboard box. Be careful not to fold it or the delicate fabric will eventually be damaged.

clean fabric (muslin or fine cotton), stapling the fabric firmly to the board. Mark out a grid, about 2 or 3 cm square, over the fabric, using a permanent marker pen (check that the ink will not run when wet or it will mark the embroidery).

Before you wet the embroidery, check that the fabric and threads are colourfast and that the fabric was pre-shrunk. If the piece can be soaked, soak it in cold water, otherwise it will have to be stretched dry. If the stitches are flat, lay the piece face down on the board; if the embroidery is raised, lay it face up to prevent crushing the threads.

Place the embroidery on the board and gently stretch it to shape, using the grid as a guide. Hold it in place with rust-free tacks or drawing pins placed close together. Let the piece dry naturally and then remove it from the board. Badly distorted pieces may need to have the process repeated several times.

FRAMING EMBROIDERY

One of the most effective ways to display your embroidery is to have it framed and then hang it on the wall. Choose a framer who specialises in embroidery for the best result.

STORING EMBROIDERED PIECES

Textiles will deteriorate almost as quickly when they are stored away as when they are in use (as long as they are used carefully) and so there is no reason not to have your embroidery on display. However, if embroidered pieces really do need to be stored away for any length of time, there are a few simple guidelines to follow.

- Store the piece flat or rolled, right side out, and wrapped in light fabric such as muslin or in an acid-free tissue paper. Do not wrap it in plastic as this will trap any moisture.
- Pieces should be stored flat if at all possible. Try to avoid folding them as the fabric and threads will become weakened where they are creased. If the piece is large and must be folded, take it out every three months or so, give it a good shake and refold it along different lines.
- Place it in a dark, dry place, such as a cardboard box or a cupboard.
- Protect the embroidered piece against moths by including a repellent such as moth balls in the storage area, but do not let them come into direct contact with the embroidered piece.

Materials and equipment

FABRICS

Fabrics used for embroidery are usually divided into two kinds: plainweave and evenweave fabrics. Plain, tightly woven fabrics of linen, cotton or silk are suitable for most surface stitchery.

Evenweave fabrics, also known as canvas, are made from wool, linen, cotton, hemp or jute in a regular grid of various sizes so that threads can be easily counted. They have an equal number of warp and weft threads per 10 cm and the gauge or size of the canvas is expressed as a number of intersecting threads per 10 cm, or this number is divided by four and expressed as threads per inch.

Canvas comes in two types. Mono canvas has a single mesh construction and Penelope or double mesh canvas is finer and has pairs of threads intersecting horizontally and vertically. They provide a secondary grid for half-size stitches, an advantage for working fine details. Canvas is used for embroidery such as cross stitch, tapestry or needlepoint. Traditionally, linen has been the most popular fabric for all types of embroidery.

Some of the specific fabrics used for the projects in this book are:

■ *Linen.* An evenweave fabric woven from flax. The threads are easily counted.
■ *Handkerchief linen.* A very fine linen.
■ *Aida fabric.* This evenweave fabric is woven into blocks to give squares for stitching. It comes in a variety of colours and is referred to by the number of squares per inch: 11, 14, 16 and 18 count or squares to the inch. It is also available in a band (sometimes called Ribband) in different counts and widths.
■ *Hardanger fabric.* An evenweave fabric with double threads. It has 9 squares to 1 cm or 22 to 1 inch.
■ *Cotton batiste.* A fine, plainweave cotton.
■ *Cotton sateen.* A glossy cotton fabric woven to resemble satin.
■ *Cotton voile.* A light, semi-transparent fabric used for shadow work.
■ *Homespun cotton.* A plainweave cotton fabric is made to resemble the fabric made at home.
■ *Muslin.* A fine, plainweave cotton fabric.
■ *Waffle cotton.* Cotton fabric woven with deep indentations on both sides to resemble a waffle.
■ *Damask.* A reversible plainweave fabric with the pattern woven into it in the same colour. It can be of silk or linen.
■ *Silk.* Plainweave fabric made from the soft, lustrous fibre produced by the silkworm to form its cocoon.
■ *Organza.* A thin, stiff fabric that can be made of silk, cotton, nylon or other fibres.
■ *Satin.* Plainweave silk or rayon fabric closely woven to show mainly warp threads and passed through rollers giving a glossy appearance.
■ *Congress cloth.* An evenweave fabric with single threads. It has 10 threads to 1 cm or 25 to 1 inch.

THREADS

A number of different threads are used for embroidery, depending on the fabric and the stitches chosen. Those used in this book include:

■ Stranded embroidery cotton (also called stranded embroidery floss) is the thread most often used for embroidery. It comes in a skein of approximately 8 m and each skein contains six strands. Stranded cotton should be used in lengths of no more than

Damask, with its subtle woven patterns, is an attractive base for the heavier types of embroidery such as this ribbon work. It is named for the city of Damascus in Syria where it was first made.

One strand of stranded silk thread—a very fine but strong thread—is used to produce this flower design, while gold metallic thread is used for the highlights.

about 40 cm or the thread loses its sheen. One or more strands can be used, depending on the fineness of the work. It is popular for many types of embroidery, including counted cross stitch, shadow work, cutwork and all types of surface stitchery. Stranded floss is also available in silk or rayon.

■ Coton Perlé, or pearl cotton, is a 2-ply thread made from cotton and is available in skeins or balls. A shiny thread, it is twisted so that it won't separate as you stitch. It comes in a variety of thicknesses: Perlé 3, 5, 8 and 12 (3 is the thickest). It is used for many types of embroidery, including tapestry and hardanger.

■ Broder cotton is a very soft, twisted (non-divisible) thread suitable for all types of embroidery. Numbers 16 and 20 are available in a range of colours but the finer 25 only in white or ecru.

■ Flower thread is a non-divisible cotton yarn with very low sheen. It is popular for cross stitch on linen.

■ Variegated thread is a stranded cotton dyed in shades of one colour by methods such as tie-dyeing.

■ Overdyed thread is dyed more than once, one colour over another.

■ Silk thread is very strong and fine but it catches easily, for example on rough hands.

■ Tapestry wool (yarn) is a twisted 4-ply yarn used for embroidery and needlepoint.

■ Crewel wool (yarn) is a fine, 2-ply yarn used for crewel embroidery and needlepoint.

■ Metallic thread is used only for special effects but is available in many weights and textures. True metallic threads come in gold, silver, copper and aluminium but today synthetic threads are also produced and are more commonly used.

■ Machine thread is a very fine thread in cotton, silk or polyester.

■ Beading or quilting cotton is stronger than normal machine thread and is less likely to break.

NEEDLES

Among the needles used for embroidery are the types listed below that are used in the projects in this book.

■ Crewel needles are sharp, pointed needles used for work on fine fabrics. They are the needles used for most embroidery. Sizes range from 1 to 10 (1 is the largest). The larger the number, the finer the needle.

■ Tapestry needles, with a blunt end, are used for work on evenweave fabrics. They come in a variety of sizes, from 14 to 26, with 14 the largest.

■ Chenille needles are sharp, pointed needles, thicker and longer than crewel needles. They have a large eye for thick threads. The sizes are from 14 to 26, which is the smallest.

■ Straw needles have a straight shaft that does not taper as most needles do.

■ Quilting needles or 'betweens' are short, fine needles with a small, round eye. They come in sizes 1 to 10, with 1 the largest.

■ Beading needles are very long, fine needles with a small eye, used for threading beads. They bend easily and so should be used carefully.

EMBROIDERY FRAMES

Embroidery frames are used to keep the work stretched tight for stitching. Most common are hoops, which consist of two rings, a smaller ring over which the fabric is placed and an outer ring that goes over the fabric and has a metal adjustable screw to fix it in place. It is a good idea to wind cotton tape around the hoops before you start stitching as an added precaution against the hoop marking the fabric.

Stretcher frames are less common but are used for large pieces of work. They consist of two pairs of stretchers that slot together to form a square frame.

Stitch library

Algerian eyelet (star stitch)

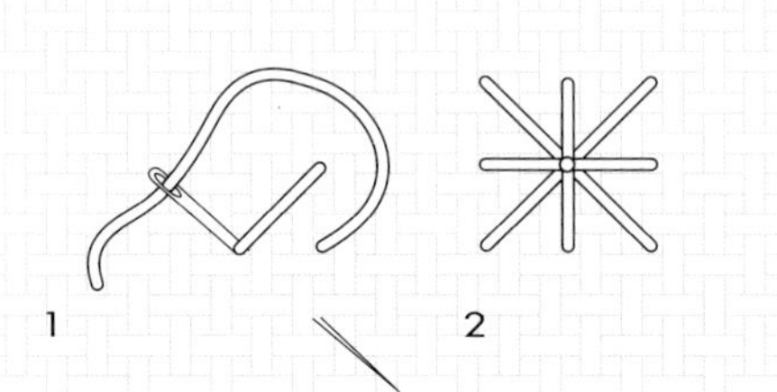

Back stitch

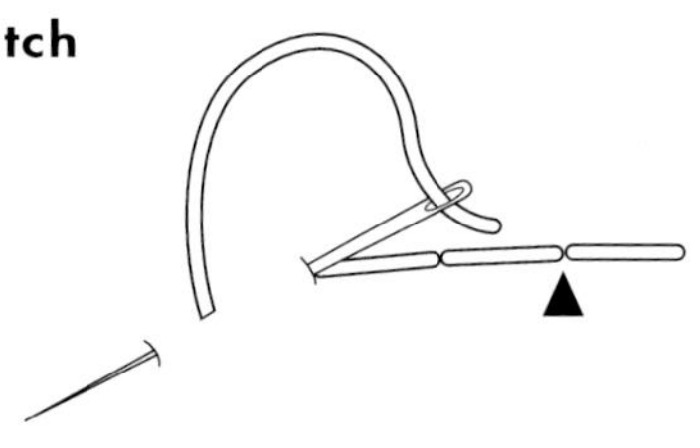

Braid stitch

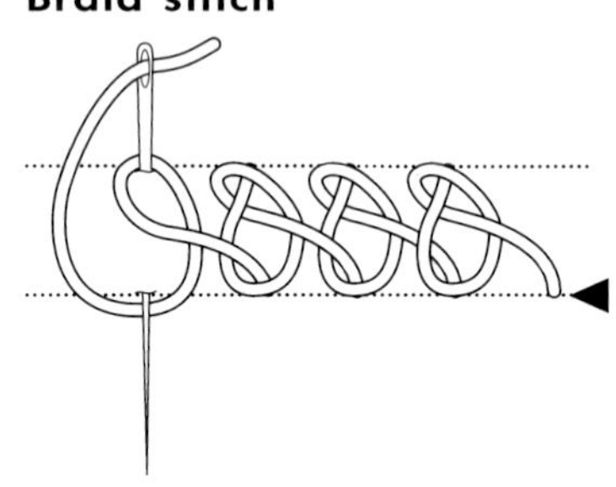

Bullion stitch

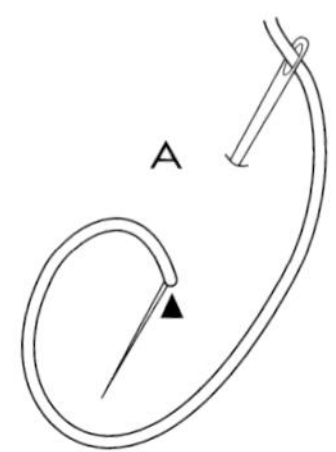

1 Pick up fabric the size of the knot

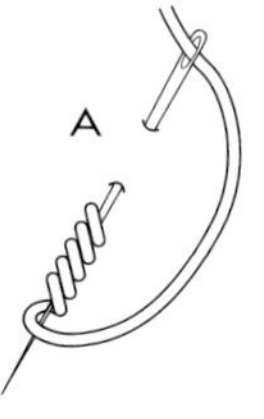

2 Twist thread around needle

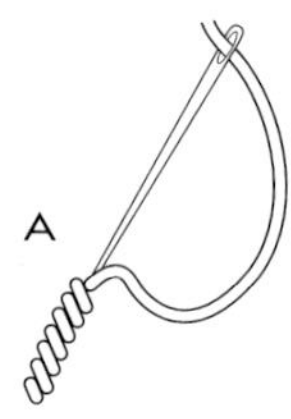

3 Pull needle through and insert again at A

Buttonhole stitch

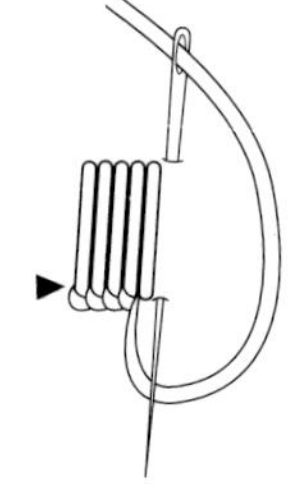

Buttonholed eyelet stitch

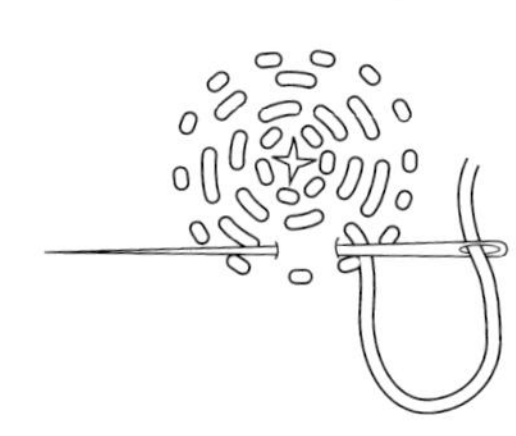

1 Work running stitches in circle and cut hole

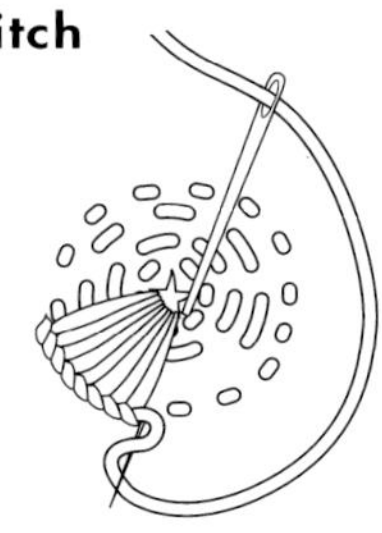

2 Work buttonhole stitches over running stitches

Cable stitch

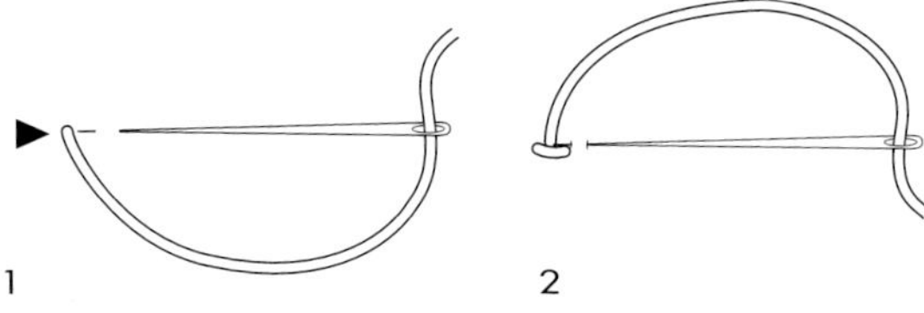

1

2

3

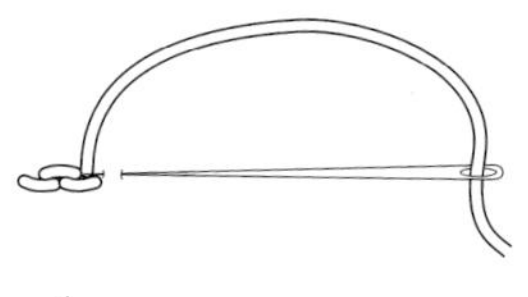

4

Chain stitch

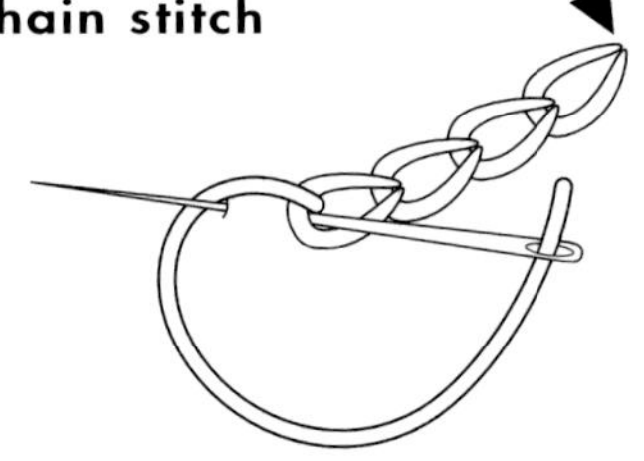

Closed herringbone stitch

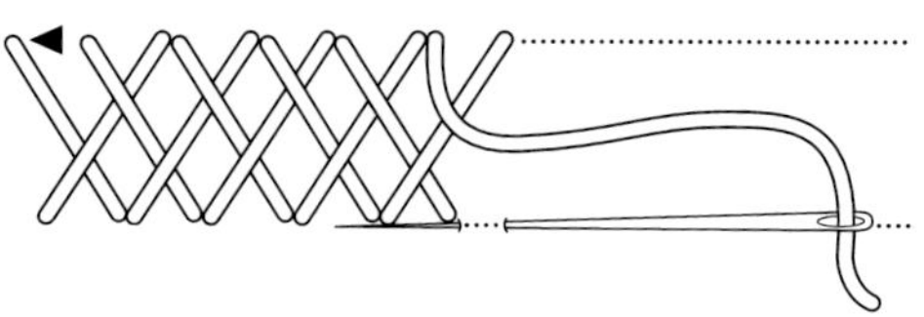

Colonial knot

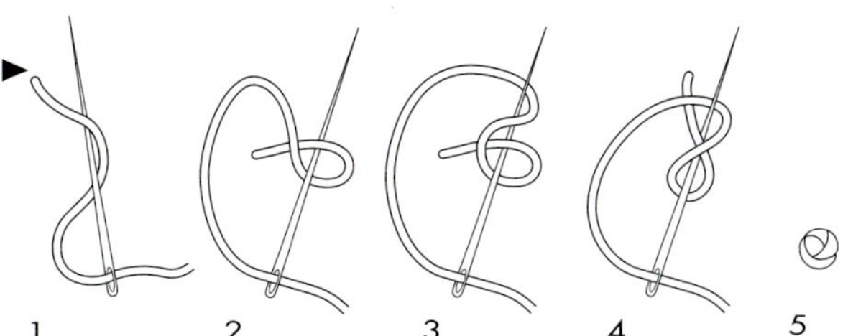

Continental stitch

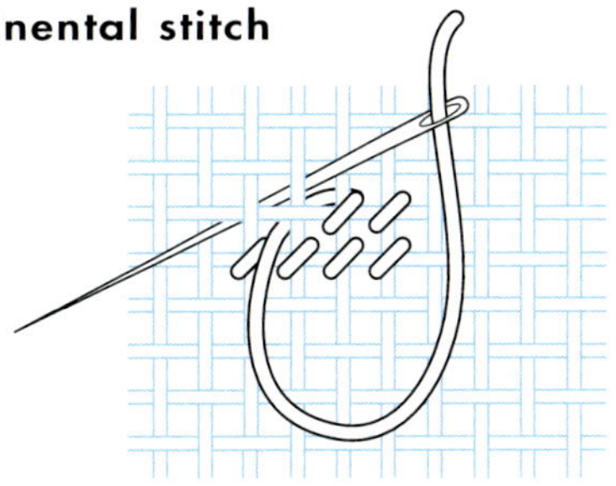

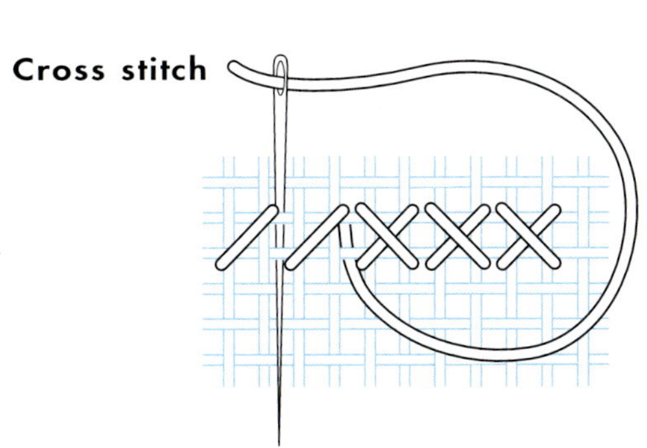

Coral knot stitch

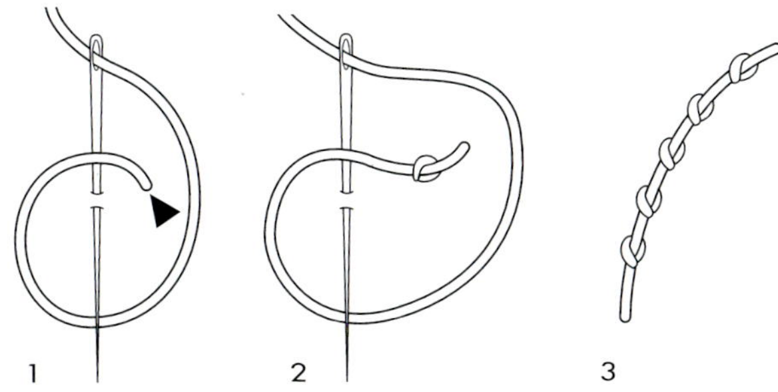

Cross stitch

Cutwork eyelet

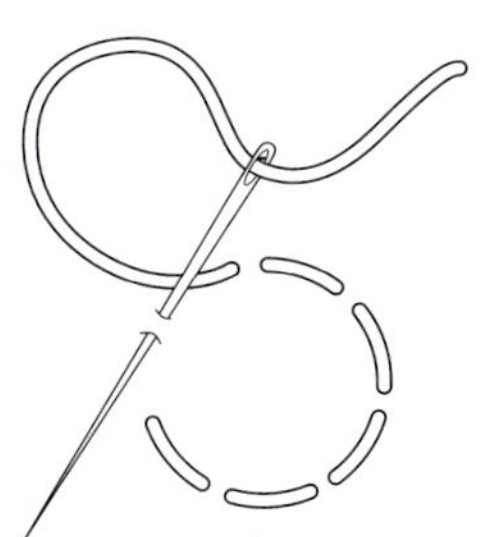

1 Work a circle of running stitches

2 Cut fabric in centre of stitches

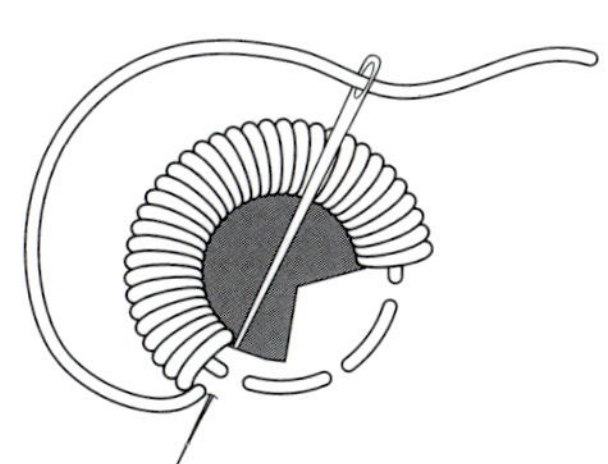

3 Work satin stitches over running stitch

Detached chain stitch (lazy daisy)

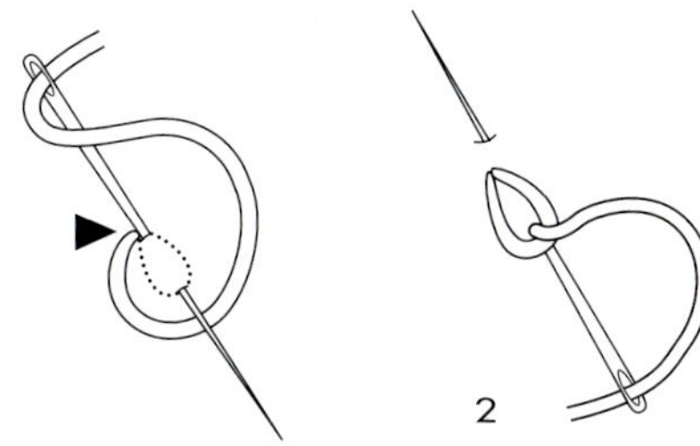

Double back stitch (shadow stitch)

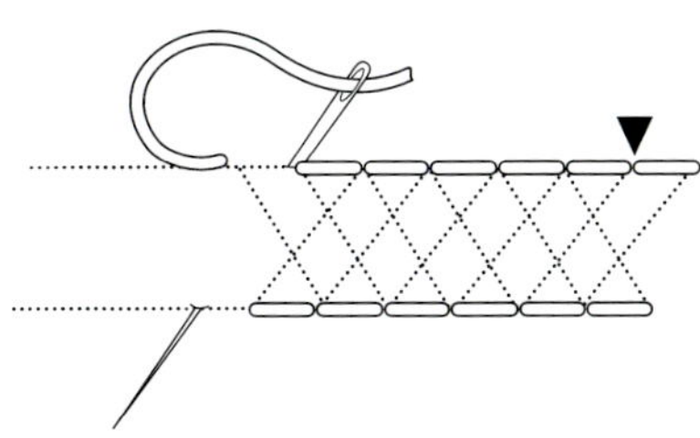

Double buttonhole stitch

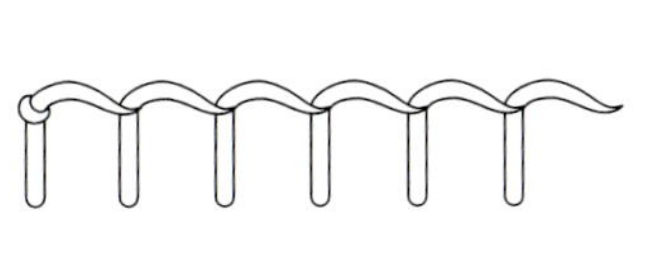

1 Work a row of buttonhole stitches one thread's width apart

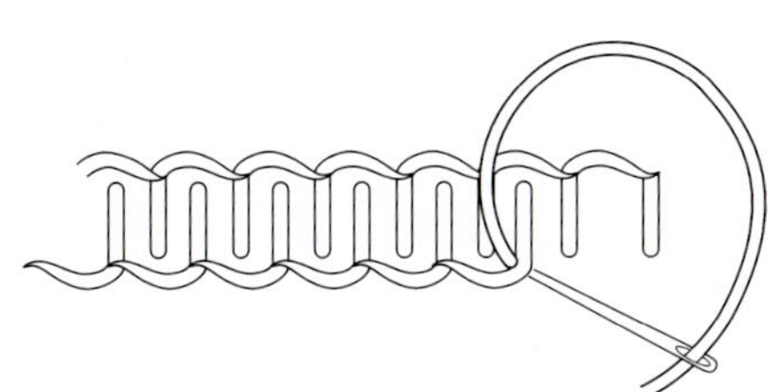

2 Turn work and make a second row in the spaces

Double feather stitch

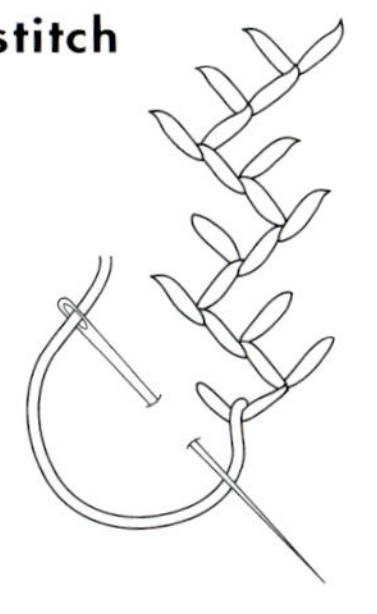

Double knot stitch

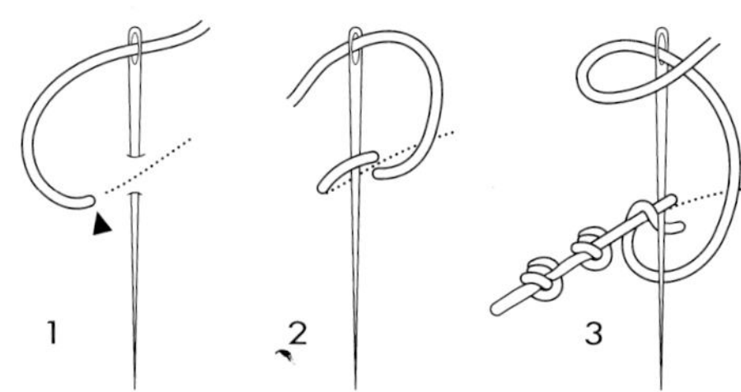

1 2 3

Eyelet stitch

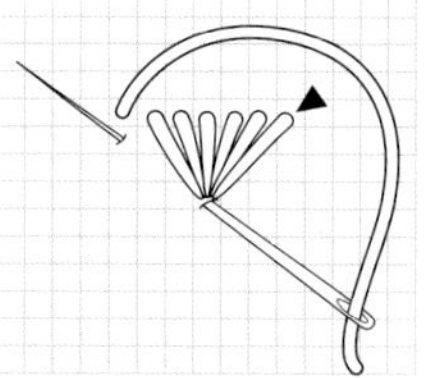

1 Bring needle up on outer edge and down in centre. Then stitch from centre out

2 Complete eyelet to form square with an even number of stitches across each side

Feather stitch

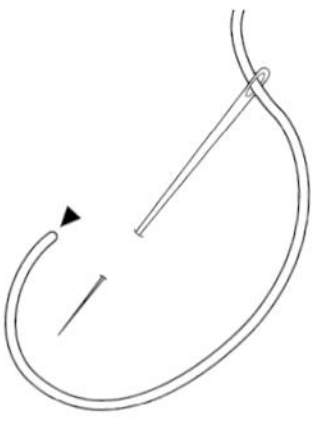

1 Keep the distance between each point the same

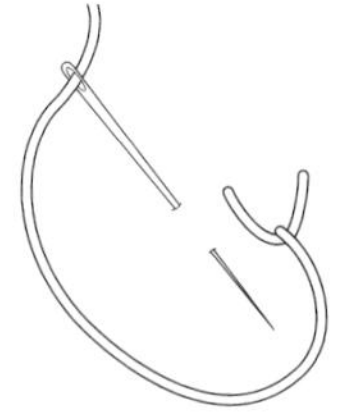

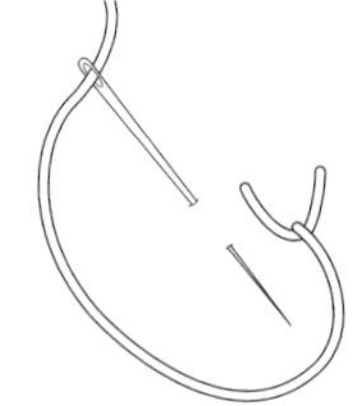

2 Reverse direction of needle for each stitch

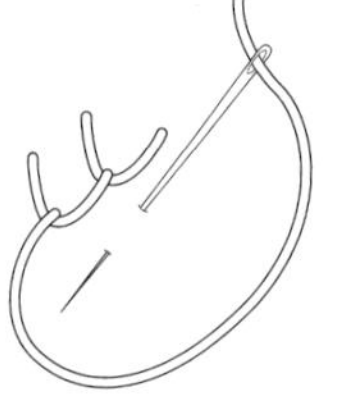

3

Fly stitch

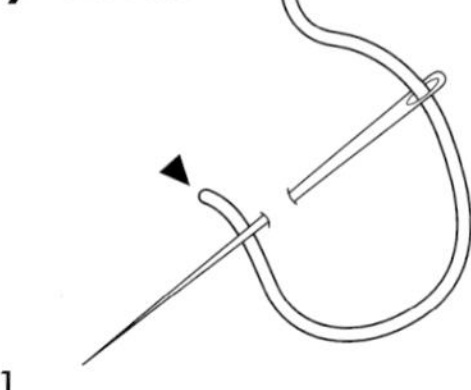

1 2

Four-sided stitch

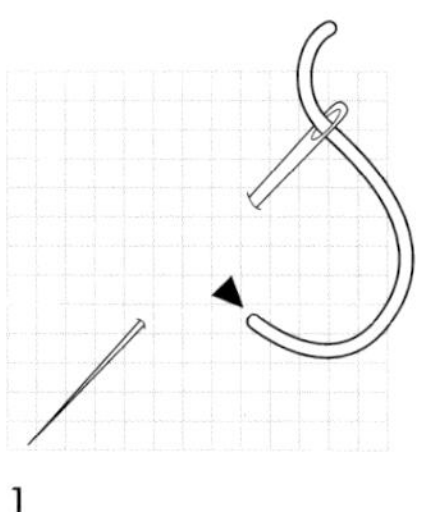

1

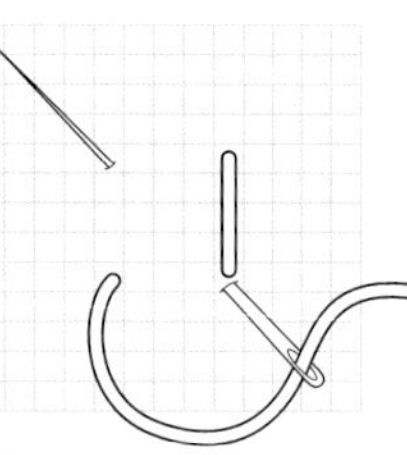

2

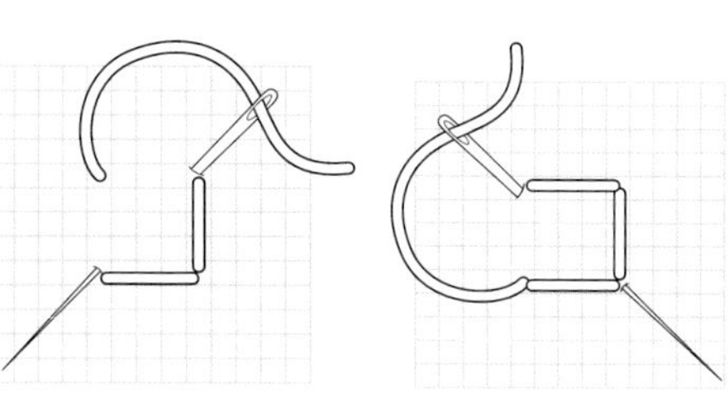

3 4

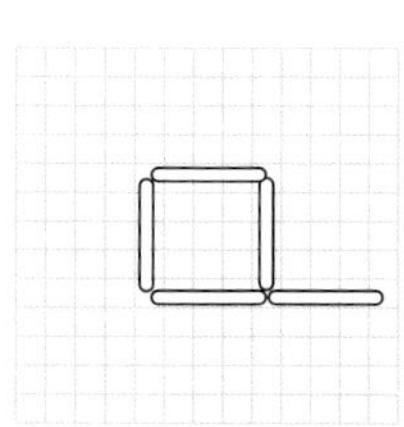

5

French knot

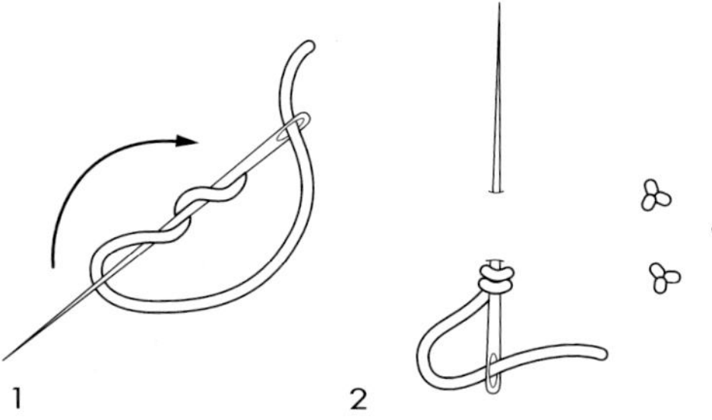

1 2

Half cross stitch

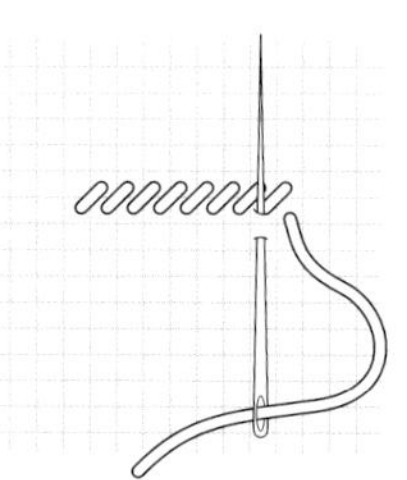

Half eyelet stitch

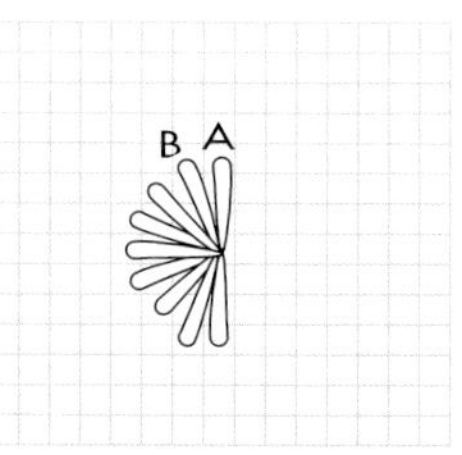

Bring needle up on outer edge and down in centre. Then stitch from centre out

Herringbone stitch

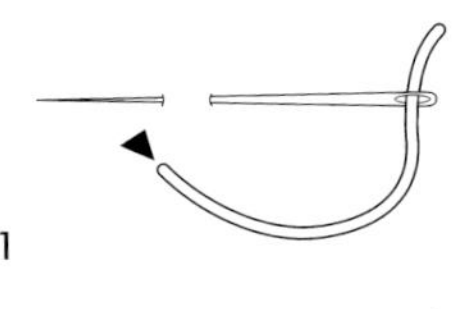

1 2

3

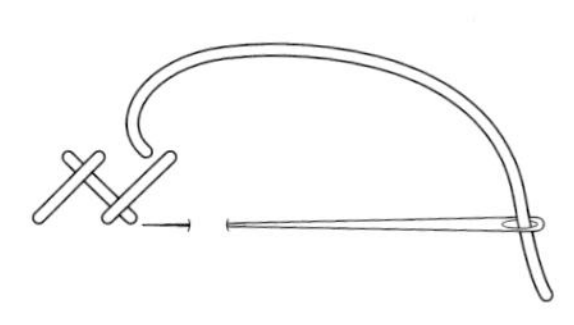

4

Honeycomb stitch

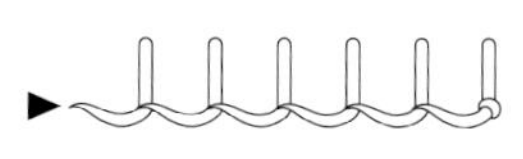

1 Work a row of buttonhole stitch, leaving loops slightly loose

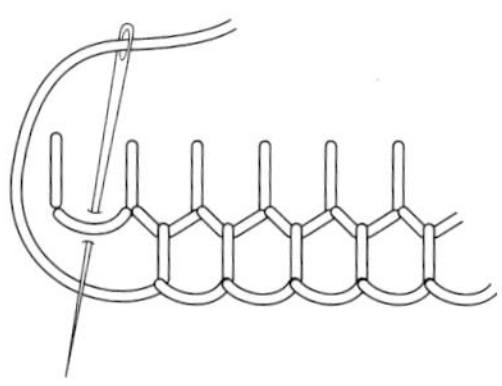

2 Work next row from right, drawing first row loops down

Ladder hem stitch

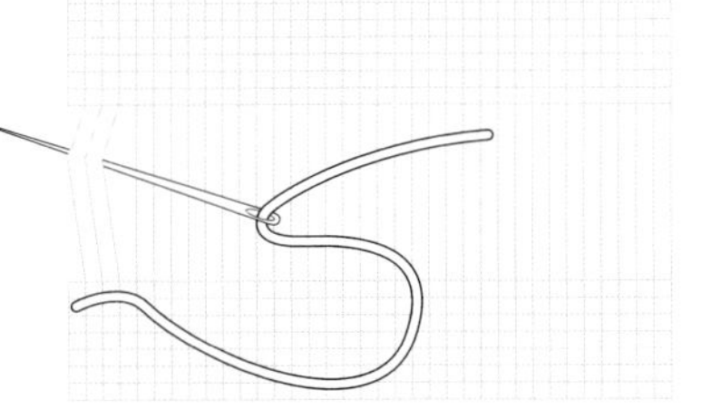

1 Work on wrong side of fabric, from left to right

2 Pass needle under a few threads

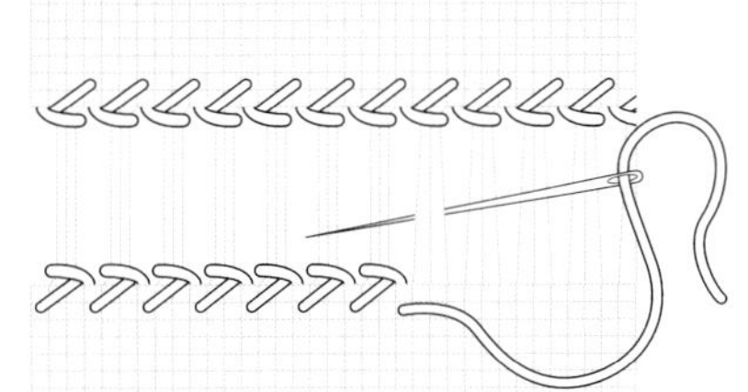

3 Turn work and repeat

Ladder stitch

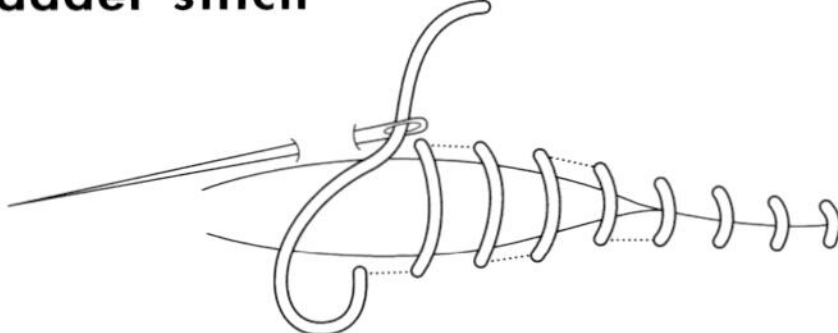

Long-legged fly stitch

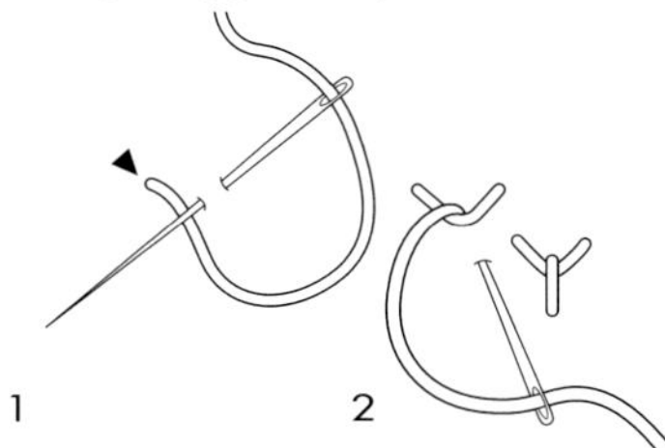

Long and short stitch

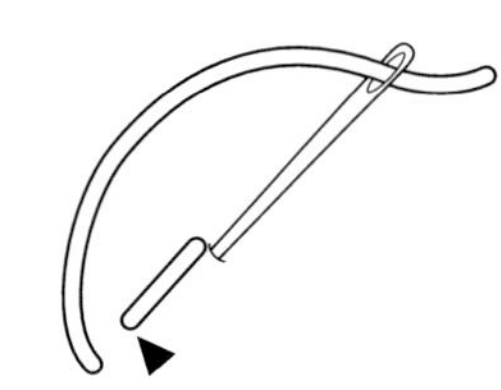

Overcast stitch

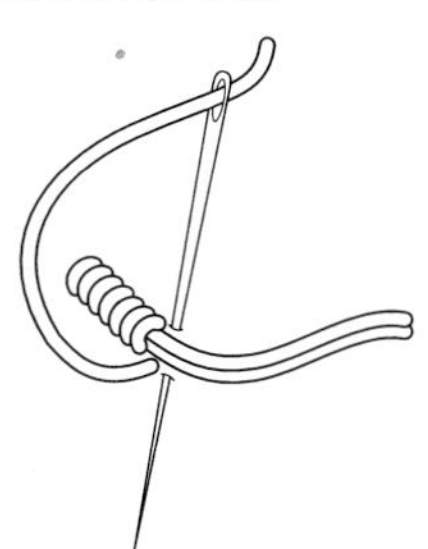

Padded satin stitch

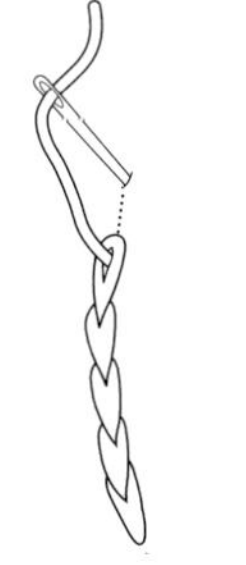
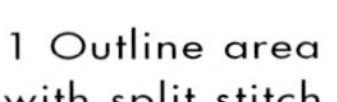

1 Outline area with split stitch

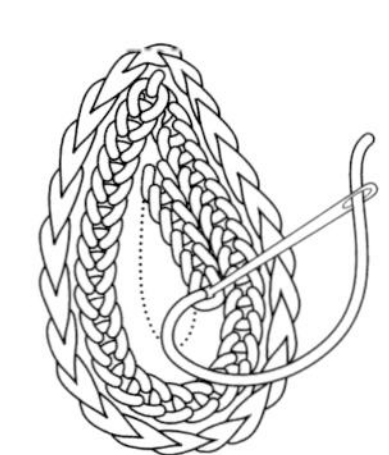

2 Fill in with chain stitch

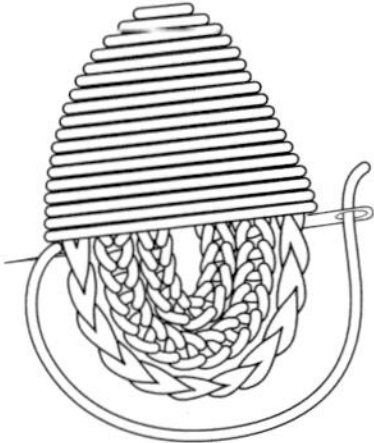

3 Cover area with satin stitch

Pistil stitch

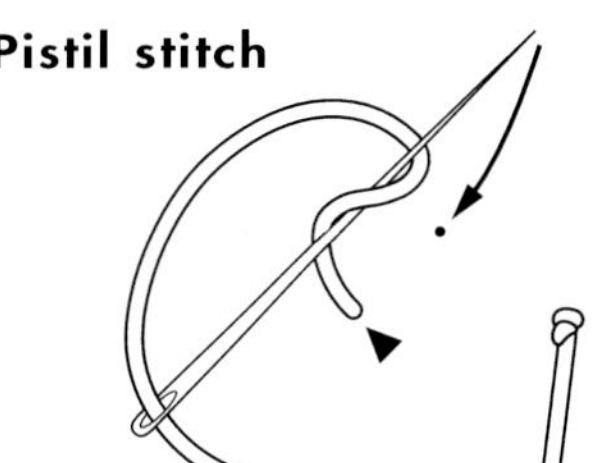

Raised stem stitch

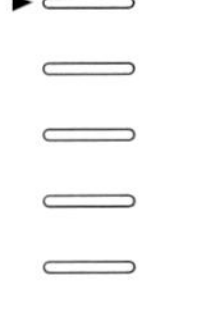

1 Work straight stitches

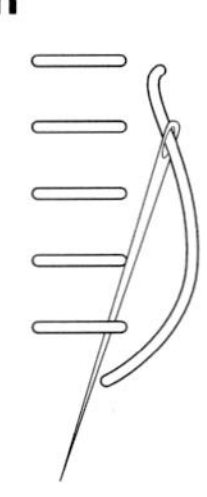

2 Work stem stitch over each stitch from bottom to top. Do not pierce fabric

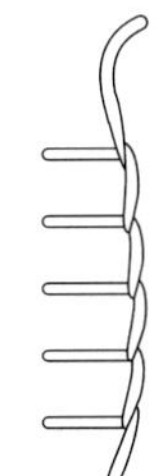

3 Again start at bottom and work to top

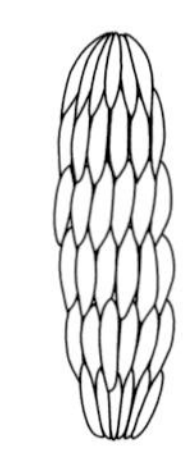

4 Completed band

Rounded eyelet stitch

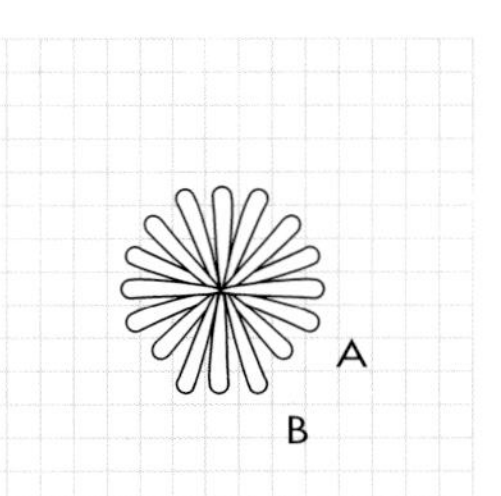

Bring needle up on outer edge and down in centre. Then stitch from centre out

Running stitch

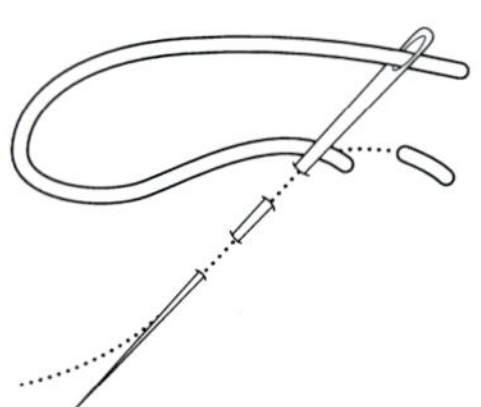

Satin stitch

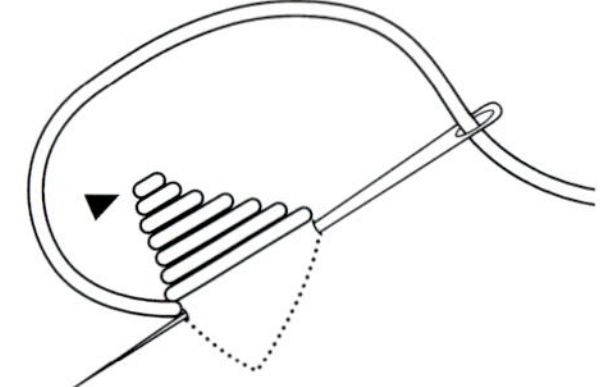

Smyrna stitch

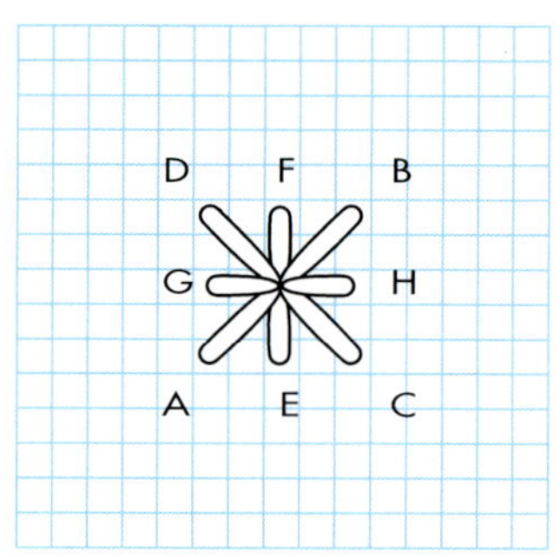

Split stitch

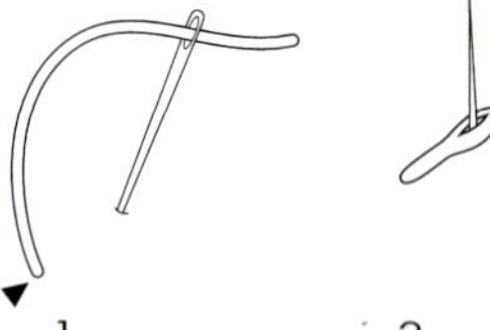

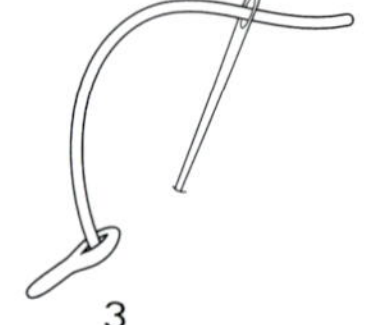

Stem stitch

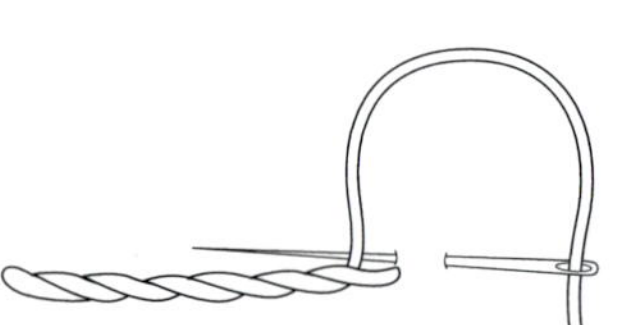

Straight stitch

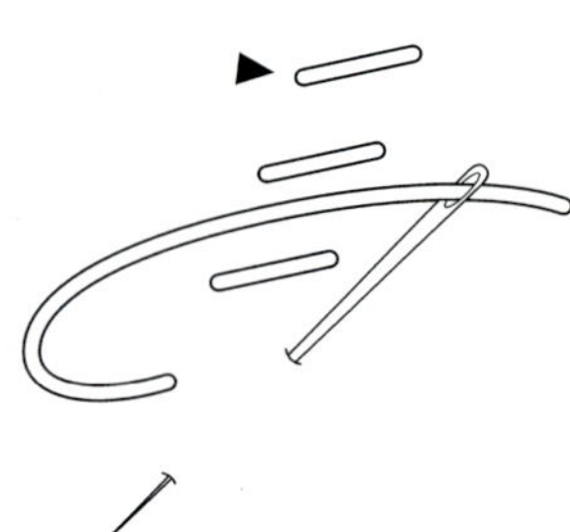

Trellis stitch with spider web

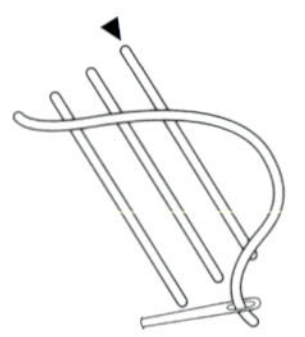

1 Cover area with parallel threads

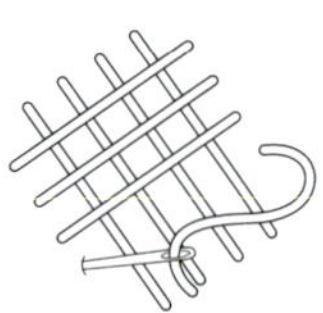

2 Work threads perpendicular to them

3 Work a small stitch over each intersection to hold it in place

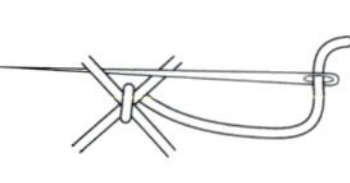

4 Weave thread over and under the four threads

5 Create webs, working across each line

Whipped back stitch

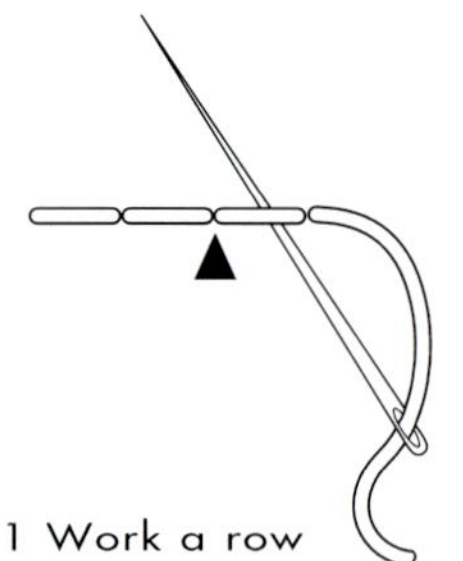

1 Work a row of stem stitch

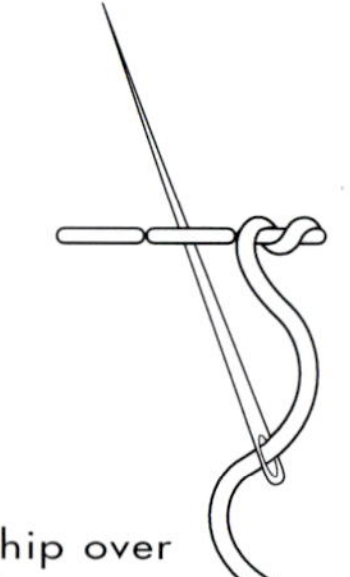

2 Whip over stitches. Do not pierce fabric

Whipped stem stitch

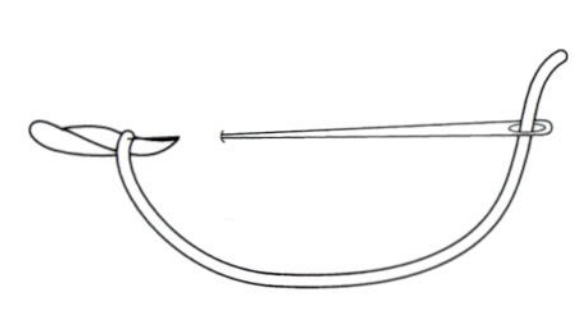

1 Work a row of stem stitch

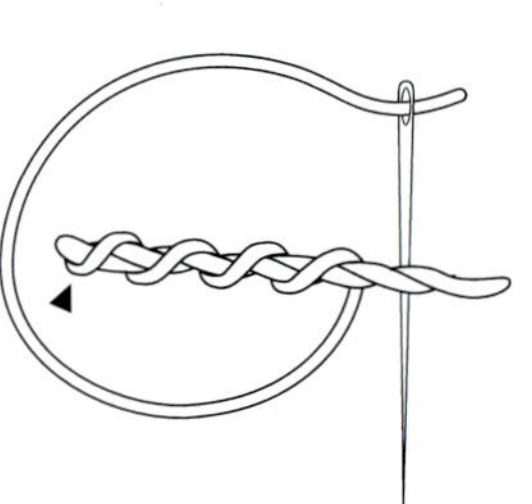

2 Whip over stitches. Do not pierce fabric

Index

A

Art Needlework, 29
Assisi embroidery, 44, 73
Ayrshire embroidery, 52, 61

B

baby wrap, 54
back stitch, 10, 13, 22, 24, 25, 43, 70, 72, 73, 90
double, 22, 25, 54, 56, 57, 58, 60, 64, 91
see also closed herringbone stitch
whipped, 78, 81, 94
bargello stitch, 73
Bayeaux Tapestry, 7, 35
beads, 32, 34, 49, 64, 65, 66, 68, 69, 70, 73, 74, 77
see also pearls
beadwork, 7, 29, 49
bed linen, 8
Berlin woolwork, 29, 35, 73
blackwork, 7
blanket, cot, 10–13
blocking, 86–7
bowl lid, 62
braid stitch, 14, 16, 90
broderie anglaise, 61
brooches, 48–9
bullion stitch, 5, 6, 10, 13, 14, 16, 31, 50, 53, 78, 80, 81, 90
buttonhole bars, 36
buttonhole fringe, 14, 16, 17
buttonhole stitch, 8, 14, 16, 17, 36, 37, 50, 53, 58, 61, 90
double, 36, 37, 91

C

cable stitch, 14, 16, 90
candlewick embroidery, 82–5
canvas work, 29, 73
Carrickmacross embroidery, 52
chain stitch, 10, 13, 14, 16, 17, 26, 28, 82, 83, 84, 85, 90
detached, 5, 6, 22, 24, 31, 39, 41, 50, 53, 82, 84, 91
christening set, 22–5
closed herringbone stitch, 26, 28, 57, 90
see also back stitch, double
coathangers, 24–5, 64–5
colonial knot, 22, 24, 48, 50, 53, 82, 84, 85, 91
continental stitch, 62, 73, 91
see also tent stitch
coral knot stitch, 14, 16, 91
couched stitches, 7, 29
crewel work, 29
cross stitch, 29, 35, 43, 44, 70, 72, 73, 91
half, 32, 34, 92
cushions, 26–8, 44
cutwork, 35, 61
see also Hardanger embroidery; Richelieu cutwork

E

evening bag, 50–3
eyelet embroidery, 61
eyelet stitch, 35, 70, 72, 73, 92
Algerian, 43, 90
buttonholed, 36, 37, 90
cutwork, 8, 91
half, 32, 34, 92
rounded, 32, 34, 93

F

fabrics, 88
feather stitch, 54, 82, 84, 92
double, 14, 16, 91
Florentine stitch, 73
fly stitch, 5, 6, 31, 39, 41, 50, 53, 92
long-legged, 10, 12, 13, 93
four-sided stitch, 58, 60, 92
frames, embroidery, 89
French embroidery, 8
French knot, 10, 12, 13, 14, 16, 17, 18, 19, 20, 21, 31, 32, 34, 43, 49, 78, 81, 92

G–H

gros point, 73
guipure work, 52
Hardanger embroidery, 58–61
hem stitch, ladder, 8, 93
herringbone stitch, 14, 16, 92
see also closed herringbone stitch
history of embroidery, 7, 29
honeycomb stitch, 14, 16, 92
Hungarian stitch, 73

K

keepsake box, 82–5
kloster blocks, 58, 60, 61
knot stitch
double, 14, 16, 92
see also colonial knot; French knot

L

lace, 34
ladder stitch, 10, 13, 22, 25, 64, 65, 93
lazy daisy *see* chain stitch, detached
lingerie bag, 74–7
long and short stitch, 5, 6, 29, 47, 50, 52, 53, 93

M

machine embroidery, 29
medieval embroidery, 7
Montmellick embroidery, 14–17, 52
mosaic stitch, 32, 34

N

needle weaving, 58, 60
needlepoint, 62, 73
needles, 7, 89
nightgowns, 31, 66–9

O

openwork, 61
opus anglicanum, 7
opus pulvinarium, 73
or nué, 7
organza cushions, 26–8
overcast stitch, 14, 16, 93

P–Q

pearls, 50, 52, 53
see also beads
petit point, 73
pictures, embroidered, 18–21, 32–4, 70–3
history of, 29, 35
pistil stitch, 50, 53, 93

placemat, Hardanger, 58–61
quick point, 73
quilting, 57, 76

R
ribbon embroidery, 38–41
Richelieu cutwork, 36–7, 61
ring cushion (wedding), 82–5
running stitch, 26, 28, 36, 37, 74, 76, 94

S
sachets
  handkerchief, 38–41
  scented, 5–6
samplers, 35, 43
satin stitch, 14, 16, 17, 36, 37, 47, 50, 53, 54, 56, 57, 58, 60, 61, 85, 94
  padded, 8, 93
shadow work, 57
  projects, 26–8, 54–7, 64–5
  see also trapunto shadow work
shoe stuffers, 78–81
smocking, 66–9
Smyrna cross, 32, 34
split stitch, 7, 10, 13, 14, 16, 17
star stitch *see* eyelet stitch, Algerian
stem stitch, 5, 6, 8, 10, 12, 13, 14, 16, 17, 18, 22, 24, 31, 36, 37, 47, 50, 53, 54, 56, 57, 64, 65, 82, 84, 85, 94
  raised, 39, 40, 93
  whipped, 14, 16, 94
storing embroidery, 87
straight loop stitch, 58, 60, 61
straight stitch, 10, 12, 13, 22, 24, 31, 36, 37, 43, 47, 49, 50, 53, 94
strapwork, 7
stumpwork, 29, 35

T
table setting, Hardanger, 58–61
tablecloth, 47
tapestries, 7
tent stitch, 29, 35
  see also continental stitch
threads, 88–9
throwover, 56
towels, guest, 14–17
trapunto shadow work, 57, 74–7
traycloth, 36–7
trellis stitch with spider web, 14, 16, 94

V-W
voile square, 54–7
washing embroidery, 86
wedding set, 82–5
white work, 52
  see also Montmellick embroidery
wool embroidery, 10–13
  see also Berlin woolwork

Published by Murdoch Books®, a division of Murdoch Magazines Pty Ltd,
213 Miller Street, North Sydney NSW 2060

Managing Editor, Craft & Gardening: Christine Eslick
Designer: Michèle Lichtenberger
Photographer: Andre Martin
Stylist: Louise Owens
Illustrators: Sonya Naumov; Lorenzo Lucia (Stitch Library and fold-out sheets)
Projects designed and stitched by Bonnie Arthurson (p. 54); Jennifer Campbell (pp. 4, 46, 48, 50, 62); Phyllis Close (p. 30); Jenny Jansen (pp. 36, 66); Juniper Designs (p. 70); Marianne Porteners (pp. 8, 26, 42); Ragnhild Rees (pp. 10, 18, 22, 32, 58, 64); Stella Robinson (pp. 44, 82); Pamela Strudwick (pp. 14, 38, 74, 78)

CEO & Publisher: Anne Wilson
International Sales Manager: Mark Newman

National Library of Australia
Cataloguing-in-Publication Data
Heirloom embroidery. Includes index. ISBN 0 86411 550 4
1. Embroidery. I. Title. II. Title: Better Homes and Gardens (Sydney, N.S.W.). 746.44

Printed by Prestige Litho, Queensland

First published 1997

Murdoch Books® is a trade mark of Murdoch Magazines Pty Ltd. Australian distribution to supermarkets and newsagents by Gordon & Gotch Ltd, 68 Kingsgrove Road, Belmore, NSW 2192. Distributed in the UK by Australian Consolidated Press (UK) Ltd, 20 Galowhill Road, Brackmills, Northampton NN4 7EE. Enquiries: 01604 760456. Distributed in NZ by Golden Press, a division of HarperCollins Publishers, 31 View Road, Glenfield, PO Box 1, Auckland 1.
*Better Homes and Gardens® (Trade Mark) Regd T.M. of Meredith Corporation

Every effort has been made to ensure the availability of materials in this book, but the availability of particular colours and fabrics cannot be guaranteed.